Summary Bundle: Business &

Life | Readtrepreneur

Publishing: Includes Summary

of The $100 Startup &

Summary of The 33 Strategies

of War

ABBEY BEATHAN

Legal & Disclaimer

3

provided by this guide. This disclaimer applies to any damages or injury caused by the use and application, whether directly or indirectly, of any advice or information presented, whether for breach of contract, tort, negligence, personal injury, criminal intent, or under any other cause of action.

You agree to accept all risks of using the information presented inside this book. You need to consult a professional medical practitioner in order to ensure you are both able and healthy enough to participate in this program.

Table of Contents

PROLOGUE

A MANIFESTO

THIS SERVES AS YOUR GUIDE TO ACHIEVE EVERYTHING YOU WANT.

Imagine yourself doing all the things you want to do, anytime and anywhere you want. You are free to pursue your dreams, your passions, and your goals. You work according to your own schedules. You work to build wealth in your own home office. You are your own boss. You travel, you rest, you sleep, and you wake up whenever you want to.

Every day, many people around the world are doing the things you imagine. They are rewriting the conventional rules of work and revolutionizing the microbusiness model. They are the unexpected entrepreneurs who suddenly find themselves doing business while crafting what they love. They live life with freedom and purpose. And yes, with huge earnings.

If you want to become one of them, let this book be your guide and compass. Learn how **freedom** and **value** can take you to your ultimate dreams.

Journey to Freedom

It all began with Chris' unexpected stumble to freedom. He never planned to become an entrepreneur. He only knew that he didn't want to work for someone else anymore. He started watching the methods used by successful people while living in one of Memphis, Tennessee cheap apartments. He reverse-engineered and applied them in his first venture-selling imported Jamaican coffee online. Then, he listed what he wanted to do and figured out how to make them come true. Soon, Chris gained one thing that was more precious than money- **freedom**. He began studying how real businesses work. He never allowed his work schedule to interfere in his freelancing job as a jazz musician at night or his reading time in cafes during the day. One day, Chris realized that he wanted to contribute to the greater good in the world, so he went to West Africa and volunteered in a medical charity for four years. He learned how to combine freedom with responsibility. When Chris returned to the United States, he started his career as a writer. He traveled and visited 20 different nations in a year and operated his business wherever he was. **Freedom** has become his compass.

Value Doctrine

Value is what you give to people when you share your

product or service. Value is the key to success of many entrepreneurs. They act on something they love- a passion, skill, or hobby and turn it into a real business. Setting up a business is easy nowadays. You don't need a big capital to start your own business. You can market your idea, product, or service instantly through various social media forms. Setting up a PayPal or other payment methods is easy, too. The modern technology and the world wide web are your amazing tools.

Read how various people in this book started their own successful business without borrowing money from the bank or studying a business course. They just followed their passion, used their skills, took risks, and created VALUE.

A Blueprint to Freedom

This book is the blueprint of Chris and people's quest for freedom- personal and financial. Some of these people are born renegades but many are ordinary folks who just want to work without restrictions that are imposed by other people. Each of them has lessons to share which you can replicate to create your own success story.

It will teach you why you need to do excellent work and keep improving. Your goal is to build a legacy by building a brand that provides VALUE to other people. You will be creating something precious and beautiful while charting your way to personal freedom.

The Book at a Glance

This book is for people who are looking for a nudge to help them make a life-changing decision.

What to Expect:

Chapter 1 talks about microbusiness and how to start one by utilizing your inherent skills.

Chapter 2 tells you why it is important to focus on value or the core benefits of your product or service.

Chapter 3 helps you discern which passion or hobby is worth the risk of pursuing.

Chapter 4 shows you why and how roaming entrepreneurs earn more and enjoy life better. Learn the business of self-publishing.

Chapter 5 discusses the new demographics which can help you understand your customers better. Use the decision-making matrix if you have many brilliant ideas.

Chapter 6 teaches you how to make a one-page business plan, why you need to launch your business as soon as you can and get your first sale.

Chapter 7 will guide you on how to create a killer offer that makes people willing to pay to get it. Learn how to nudge your customers to make an urgent decision to buy.

Chapter 8 teaches you how to launch your product or service in a Hollywood style.

Chapter 9 provides reasons why hustling is an art.

Chapter 10 teaches you about money- how to earn it through business and how to start a venture without spending too much.

Chapter 11 is about tweaks or small actions that bring in big profits.

Chapter 12 shows you how to self-franchise.

Chapter 13 is about going long and growing your business.

Chapter 14 shows you reasons why you should not be afraid to fail because it usually opens a new path to success.

PART I

UNEXPECTED
ENTREPRENEURS

Chapter 1

Renaissance

You already have the skills you need—you just have to know where to look.

Michael Hanna lost his sales job of 25 years on May 4, 2009. The 360-degrees turnaround of his career knocked him hard. After the shocking episode, he decided to face the reality and search job leads. It was a tough hunt. One day, a friend of Martin who manufactured mattresses asked him to sell the remaining pieces. He accepted the offer, told his wife Mary Ruth about the plan, and looked for a shop. He found one in the city. Martin used Craigslist to sell the first inventory. The sale went well. His only problem was how to answer the customers' questions of what type of mattress they were buying. He decided to learn more about mattresses. He made a deal with the shop's landlord and talked to local suppliers. His wife built a business website. When he offered a delivery service by bicycle, Martin's business became a hit in Portland. Martin never expected that he would be managing his own store and that it would provide more than enough money for his family.

Around the world, many ordinary people are establishing

their businesses via the Internet. Bloggers, influencers, coaches, online teachers, and other creative people chose to operate online micro-businesses independently. They opted to turn their passions into profitable ventures. They followed their own schedules and created meaningful lives for themselves.

The $100 Startup Business Model

As writer-entrepreneur, Chris had access to lots of case studies on microbusiness. He also operated a series of this type of business. Piqued with curiosity, he began a comprehensive study and talked to his colleagues and friends. He collaborated with *"Escape from Cubicle Nation"* author Pamela Slim and produced a low-budget workshop series in 2010. In a matter of 90 minutes, the first workshop was sold-out. They offered slots for another future workshop, and the same thing happened. There was a huge demand.

Chris liked the *"follow-your-passion"* idea that catapulted small businesses into great empires. He interviewed successful entrepreneurs around the world and compiled their stories in his online course – the *Empire Building Kit*. The course inspired him to launch a bigger project, and also write *"The $100 Startup"* book.

He collected data from respondents across the globe and listened to accidental entrepreneurs during his book tours in North America. He established 6 criteria to gather the necessary case studies.

1. Follow-your-passion model
2. Low startup cost
3. No special skills
4. At least $50,000 a year in net income
5. Fewer than five employees
6. Full financial disclosure

The case studies that are presented in this book are stories of people who jumpstart their microbusinesses without much idea of what they were doing, without a big investment, without a formal business plan, without market testing, and without employees. Like Michael, these people began their journey to entrepreneurship after a difficult circumstance.

Chris called their stories as an *ensemble* – individual voices that became an original composition. His goal in sharing the stories is to provide a blueprint for your own escape plan and gain financial, personal freedom.

3 Lessons of Successful Business

Lesson 1: Convergence

It is the intersection between what you like or care about and what is interesting for other people that they will spend money to get it.

Lesson 2: Skill Transformation

Many businesses are built using related skills, not exactly the necessary skills. To make your business successful, utilize the skill or combination of skills that would help your potential clients.

Lesson 3: The Magic Formula

The secret of microbusiness alchemy – Passion/Skill + Usefulness = SUCCESS.

What to Learn

The basics of building business are:

- *Product or Service* - what you will sell
- *People who are willing to pay* – your customers

- *A way to get paid* – to exchange your product or service for money

Once you established these three factors, you are in business. The next move is to *ramp up* sales and profit. It is necessary to think of a strategy to attract attention and build interest among potential customers. You also need to maintain the current list of people who patronize your product or service.

KEY POINTS

- Microbusinesses are not new concepts.

- To start a business, you need to have 3 things- a product/service, people waiting to pay to get it, and a way to get paid. Others are optional.

- Skill transformation is about applying knowledge to create new projects.

- Merge your skill and passion to create something that is useful for other people.

Chapter 2

Give Them the Fish

How to put happiness in a box and sell it?

The key principle to build a path to freedom is to start a microbusiness that is based on your passion, hobby, or skill. The quickest way to start your business is to know what people want and find a way to supply it.

Kelly Newsome

Kelly was a high-paying lawyer in Manhattan. After 5 years of practice, she wanted a change. She joined Human Rights Watch, an international charity which provided her a sense of fulfillment. While working there, Kelly realized that she wanted to start something on her own. She also liked to travel the world and pursue her passion for yoga. She enrolled in a 200-hour Yoga training course, then, taught about it in Europe and Asia. Her next step was to establish the Higher Ground Yoga in Washington, D.C. She focused on 30-45-year old lady executives in the corporate world, pregnant women, and mothers with little children. Within a year, Kelly was able to reach $50,000+ income level and an annual bracket of $85,000. Though she suffered a loss during the East Coast snowpocalypse, Kelly opted to keep the business going. Kelly discovered that the secret of a meaningful career is to make people always feel good.

IDEAS & OPPORTUNITIES

When you start thinking like an entrepreneur, you notice ideas and opportunities for your microbusiness wherever you go.

Here are some inspirations:

- Not finding something you want in the market
- There is a changing space.
- An opportunity when there is a new technology.
- Side projects, offshoots, and related projects.

Important tip: Always equate your business idea with money.

1. How much will I earn?
2. How can they pay me?
3. Are there ways that can help me earn more than once?

What Is Value?

Value is defined as the regard that something is deemed to deserve. May also mean importance or uselessness of something. In the context of this book, *value* becomes a way to help people. *Freedom* motivated Kelly to put up Higher Ground Yoga but the *value* she provided for her clients became the key to her success.

Instead of talking about the features of your product or service, give more time discussing the benefits or *values* that it provides. The more you connect with customers' emotions, the greater is the sales income.

Strategies

Strategy 1: Find out the hidden needs

Remember that sometimes what people say and what they want are not the same things. You need to dig deeper.

Wedding photographer Kyle Hepp was known for her non-traditional shots. She always gave what her clients wanted but made sure that she had traditional shots, too. This way, everybody including the bride and groom's families was happy with her service.

Strategy 2: Find ways to make your customer a hero

Purna Duggirala offered training for people who wanted to become adept in Microsoft Excel. His income in a year was around $136,000. His clients considered him as "BFF for Excel". He chronicled tips & tutorials about Excel use, created downloadable guides, and offered ongoing online training in his website. He made work easier for clients and make them *"a hero"* in front of their co-employees and bosses.

Strategy 3: Offer what people want

Sell a product or service that people buy. Think not of what they need, and more of what they want.

Chris has a failure-to-success progression to tell. His constant travel around the world inspired him to create the *Travel Ninja* – a guide that illustrates how to travel on a budget. The initial response was okay, but he only sold a hundred copies during the launch. He was confused. Finally, he realized that customers didn't really care about complexities and details. They wanted to know how to get the cheapest deals. After a year, he decided to create another guide- the *Frequent Flyer Master*. This time, he made it simpler and more accessible. He sold 500 copies during the launching and earned $50,000+ net income. Chris made his third travel guide project- the *Travel Hacking Cartel* which tells people how to make deals around the world and take advantage of them to get free tickets. 3,000 copies were sold during the launch day. Chris finally learned how to deliver what his customers want.

Six Steps to Start Your Business

1. Decide what type of product or service you will sell.
2. Create a website.
3. Develop an offer.
4. Set-up a way to get paid.
5. Launch your business by announcing an offer.
6. Learn step 1-5, then repeat the cycle.

What People Want

Providing what the customers really want is extremely critical for any business. If your business is on giving more (love, acceptance, freedom, free time, and money) and reducing taking away (stress, uncertainty, hassle, and conflict), then, you are on the right track.

KEY POINTS

- Value is about helping people.
- Give people what they want, not what you believe they should have.
- Market the core benefits, not the features.

- Focus on what you can do to improve people's lives and get paid.

Chapter 3

Follow Your Passion ... Maybe

Get paid to do what you love by making sure it connects to what other people want.

Gary Leff, CFO to 2 university research centers of Northern Virginia and consultant of his own part-time business usually starts his day by opening e-mails. Like Chris, he is a "travel hacker" who earns and redeems miles into actual leisure vacation. Gary set up business and first-class trips for busy people based on their preferences. His service fee is $250. Business boomed when *Condé Nast Traveler* featured him. Last year, his income was around $75,000. He invests his money and cashes on miles accounts to travel with his wife around the world. Gary's story is a classic example of follow-your-passion business. He found creative ways to travel free. He provided immense value and he got paid.

Do not rush

First, you cannot pursue any passion just because you particularly enjoy it. Remember the convergence lesson? You

23

need to create a project that other people would value, something that would help them.

The *second* important principle that successful follow-your-passion entrepreneur understand is- you get paid when you pursue a hobby that helps other people.

Mignon Fogarty

She created the QDT Network and hosted the *Grammar Girl* show. The show was an instant hit and attracted media attention. It also spawned series of books and related programs. But, before her success as Grammar Girl, she did the *Absolute Science* podcast which was not very profitable. So, Mignon changed course. She didn't abandon her passion but she chose the right one that connected with the audience.

Checklist

For You:

- Do you like to pursue your passion 20 hours or more a week, instead of doing it only in your free time?
- Do you enjoy the details of your hobby?
- Do you like teaching other people?
- Will you enjoy doing the administrative work of your hobby?

For the Marketplace:

- Did other people ask you to help them?
- Are there people who want to pay for your expertise?
- Are there businesses already serving the market but not like what you can offer to them?

To turn passion into a profitable venture, it is necessary to have a skill to solve a specific problem. The merging of passion and skill to create something that people value will put money into your bank account.

(Passion + skill) → (problem + marketplace) = opportunity

Next, you have to transfer the passion into a business model. The idea is to have the right passion, sell it to the right audience, and use the right business model.

KEY POINTS

- Good business gives solutions to problems.
- Always ask- "Where is the business model?" whenever you are considering a business opportunity.
- Not all hobbies are worth pursuing.

Be more specific if you are considering a consulting business.

25

Chapter 4

The Rise of the Roaming Entrepreneur

"Location, location, location" is overrated.

Roaming entrepreneurs and digital nomads are everywhere.

Case Study: The Music Teacher

Brandon Pearce lived in Utah in 2009. He was a successful piano teacher who wanted to do more. He was curious to know how he could mix his passion with the modern technology. At first, he just wanted to find a solution to what he referred to as *"disorganized music teacher problem."* He created Music Teacher's Helper for personal use at first, then, eventually turned it into a one-stop platform where teachers could easily create their own site and handle the scheduling and billing. This allowed them to focus on what they enjoy most-teaching music.

It became a profitable business. He offered value and he charged a fee up to $588 per year. He also included a free version which can be used for a limited period. After 3 years, his life changed dramatically. He lives in Costa Rica with his family. His business has 10 remote employees from all over the world. He works 8-15 hours a week and spends the rest enjoying life with his family and pursuing other side projects that he enjoys. The Music Teacher's Helper is currently earning $360,000 annually.

Primer for Roaming Entrepreneurs

- Set up your business before roaming the world

- Frequently change the passwords of your accounts.

- Use Dropbox & Google Docs to store your work "in the cloud".

- You can stay in different countries if you have a Canadian or U.S. passport.

- Learn visa requirements of countries you want to visit.

- Two of the most hospitable and easiest regions are Southeast Asia and Latin America.

- Find low-cost places away from home at AirBnB.com or stay free via CouchSurfing.org.

- Search for tech-friendly places. Check MeetPlanGo.com or BootsnAll.com.

- When abroad, balance your work and adventure. Enjoy visiting the places and experience the local culture.

One popular business model that is useful and highly-profitable for individuals who work at any location is – information publishing.

Jack Covert is the founder of the leading business books retailer 800-CEO-READ. He is a veteran in traditional publishing who pursued self-publishing. Jack told Chris that "everything has changed" in the world of publishing. In the past, according to Jack, the majority of authors prefer to self-publish because they couldn't find traditional publishers to buy their works. Nowadays, authors have a choice to directly distribute their work and become independent. Digital publishing solved the authors' dilemma. It offered deals for one-off products, recurring subscriptions, and fixed-period courses.

One may ask if there is really a huge market space for online projects. The answer is affirmative. Self-publishing is a direct type of selling which ensures quality, speed, and potential to be read by more readers. The growth of this business greatly depends on referral.

Become Your Own Publisher

1.   Find a topic that makes people pay just to learn

about it.

2.   Share the information with written material, video or audio recording, or a combination of the two.

3.   Create an e-book, a digital package, or a product that is downloadable.

4.   Make an offer. What are you selling and why people should buy it?

5.   Decide a fair price that equates the value of your offer.

6.   Find the best method to get paid.

7.   Publish your offer. Promote it.

8.   Cash in and have fun!

KEY POINTS

- Roaming entrepreneurs who are earning six figures and above are everywhere.

- Information publishing is the most profitable business for those who prefer to work anywhere.

- Some people pursue a nomadic lifestyle for wrong reasons. Ask yourself- "What do you want to do?"

- Combine your passion and usefulness to create a real business wherever you are.

Chapter 5

The New Demographics

Your customers all have something in common, but it has nothing to do with old-school categories.

Who are your customers? Where are they? How do you find them? These questions help you identify the ideal customers and fit them into traditional demographics. However, when it becomes difficult to categorize them, put them into the new demographics.

Traditional Demographics

Age, Location, Sex/Gender, Race/Ethnicity, Income

New Demographics

Interests, Passions, Skills, Beliefs, Values

Changing the "Who"

Kris Murray was a working mom who developed a method to help child care providers run the business more efficiently. She offered it to various owners who showed lack of interest.

She persisted because Kris believed that she was on the right track. With no positive response from her target clients, she was ready to quit. But before doing it, she looked at her project again and tweaked it. First, Kris streamlined the services and made it clients-oriented. She gave what they wanted. She gave them fish. The second thing that she did was to *"change the WHO."* She looked for multi-location center owners who can afford her consulting services. Her business grew and earned $20,000 a month.

Working Strategies

If you want to follow the footsteps of successful business owners, check the following strategies:

Strategy 1: Find and Latch on to a New Craze or Passion

Jason Glaspey tried Paleo diet and adopted it as his lifestyle. However, he noticed that it was difficult to follow the diet. Jason decided to create a solution that helped him and other Paleo followers. He started Paleo Plan – a simple plan which lists down what to buy, what to cook, and what to eat weekly. Within a year, Jason was earning $6,000 a month. And he only needed 2 hours a week to work on his website's updates.

Strategy 2: Know What People Buy

There are 2 kinds of marketing: the old-school marketing which uses *persuasion* and the new marketing which extends an *invitation*. The entrepreneurs that are featured in this book use the second type of marketing. They created businesses that clients were desperate and enthusiastic to be part of.

The Customer Is Sometimes "Wrong"

At 5:00 A.M., Chris was awake to monitor his new website's launching. He was happy to see the shopping cart filling up and checking the inbox to answer support issues. He was also emailing thank-you notes to his customers. Then, he saw a note from Dan asking for a refund. Chris instantly replied yes, then, asked him what's wrong. Dan asked Chris to call him. Chris opted to continue working with his core market instead of entertaining one dissatisfied customer.

Make a "Possibilities List" and Use the "Decision-Making Matrix"

What to do when you have many ideas but no extra time to pursue them all? First, write them down and second, evaluate competing ideas. A *"possibilities list"* helps you store great ideas which you can use in the future. In evaluating ideas, you need

32

the *decision-making matrix* to separate "winning ideas" from "maybe later ideas."

The basic questions:

- Does this project produce a concrete product or service?
- Do you know people who are willing to buy it?
- Do you have a way to get paid?

The *"decision-making matrix"*

List your ideas on the left column of the matrix. Score them 1-5, 5 is the highest. Score them according to the following criteria:

- *Impact*
- *Profitability*
- *Effort*
- *Vision*

Tally them on the right-hand column. The idea is to look for trends, eliminate the lowest in the ranking and proceed with rank 1.

KEY POINTS

- Who are your people (your customers)? Think of them in terms of values and beliefs (new demographics) instead of age, gender, or race (old demographics).

- Utilize surveys to help you understand your customers and the potential prospects.

- Establish yourself as an authority and simplify the process of a popular craze or new trends.

- Use the "decision-making matrix" to help you evaluate the various ideas and decide.

PART II

TAKING IT TO THE
STREETS

Chapter 6

The One-Page Business Plan

If your mission statement is much longer than this sentence, it could be too long.

Omar Noory and Jen Adrion are both graduates of Columbus College of Art and Design in Ohio. Jen teaches at their alma mater while Omar has a design job. They are also freelance designers. After a year of making both ends meet, they experienced *"burnout"*. One day, while driving back from Chicago, they decided to talk about their upcoming New York trip which they hope would be first of many travels. Once they arrived home, they looked for a map to chart their future adventures and found nothing they liked so they made one. However, the printer only accepted a minimum order of 50 which would cost them $500. They each put $250. The output was beautiful. They hung one on their wall, gave some to friends, and decided to create a one-page website to sell the remaining 44 maps. After adding a PayPal button, they slept. When they woke up the following day, they had one buyer which led to other sales. When their website was mentioned in a popular forum, they sold all maps in just 10 minutes. They also received messages from others begging for reprint. During the next months, Jen and Omar were busy working on their ideas. They wanted to grow steadily and only made new products when there was a valid reason. Everything they do and sell should be essential. After 9 months, they quit their jobs and work full-time on their business. It brought back their passion for design.

Plan & Action

Nothing is wrong when you plan. But, don't wait too long. Take action, start quickly, and see the outcome.

Choose a selling idea. It must be useful or provide a solution to a problem. To determine if your idea will attract customers, start as soon as possible.

Keep the costs low. When you invest more sweat than money, you reduce the impact of possible failure and avoid financial loss or debt.

Make the first sale as soon as possible. To begin your success in business, get started. Set up your website and offer your project.

Market before you manufacture. Post a sample on your website and see how people respond. When there is enough demand, you can start working on your project.

Respond to the initial result. After your initial sales success, regroup and decide your next list to do. Hire the services of people or other businesses to facilitate other tasks.

And lastly, *review what brought the initial success* whether it was coincidental or accidental.

Receive & Give

Whenever you think of value and freedom, you should always focus on how your business will help other people. There are people who design their business around a social cause, others integrate social project within the business, and the rest shift the focus as they continue their operations.

The 140-Character Mission Statement

Breaking down the process of planning is quite simple. First, define your business mission statement (business idea) in 140 characters or less. Think about your product or service and your customers. Put them together and you have a mission statement.

We provide [product or service] for [customers].

Highlight the core benefit that your business provides for customers instead of descriptive features. You can revise your mission statement like this-

We help [customers] do/achieve/other verb [primary benefit].

KEY POINTS

- Launch the business as soon as possible then "plan as you go".

- Find a way to make your first sale.

- To gauge people's interest, use the Seven Steps to Instant Market Testing.

- Outline your ideas in a One-Page Business Plan.

- Make a 140-Character Mission Statement to explain your business ideas.

Chapter 7

An Offer You Can't Refuse

The step-by-step guide to creating a killer offer

It's time to create an offer that is hard to refuse. Remember the following: *First*, sell what your target customers will buy. *Second*, market it at the right time to the right people. *Finally*, craft a compelling offer.

1. Make an offer that provides what customers actually want so they pay.

2. Nobody wants to be pressured to buy something. Compel people to buy from you by creating an offer that is hard to refuse and seems like an invitation.

3. Encourage the customers to accept the offer by creating a sense of urgency that necessitates their immediate action. A gentle nudge that says – *"Do it now!"*

Tool Kit to Create Killer Offer

1. *Frequently Asked Questions (FAQ)*

This section does not only answer the questions but also provides additional assurance to future buyers and helps them overcome their objections. It's like an "operation objection busting." With FAQ, you are building authority and trust. It is necessary to build your consumer confidence in order to overcome specific and general objections. Use their objections to your advantage by turning them into positive messages like-

- *This is a great investment because* ...
- *This really works because* ...
- *You can trust us with your money because* ...

Be proactive, not defensive when you respond to customers' concerns:

2. *The Guarantee*

"What if I don't like it? Can I get my money back?" To counteract these concerns of potential buyers, you need to offer them an incredible satisfaction guarantee or not at all.

Make your guarantee offer clear and simple. If you

cannot afford to give it because it would cost you a substantial cost of delivery, then choose not to offer. The lack of customer satisfaction guarantee keeps hard to please customers away and attracts those who believe in your product or service.

3. *Over-delivering*

Give your customers more than they expect. This reinforced the feeling that they did the right thing. Over-delivering builds up your list of loyal people who patronize your product or service.

KEY POINTS

*   Connect the offer directly to the benefits that your buyers will receive.
*   Find out what the customers really want when they tell you what they want. Sometimes, it is not the same thing.
*   When you create an offer, make sure that you are addressing their objections in advance.
*   Gently nudge your customers to buy.
*   Offer acknowledgment and reassurance once they

hired your service or purchase your product. Go beyond their expectations to cement the alliance.

Chapter 8

Launch!

A trip to Hollywood from your living room or the corner coffee shop

Hollywood producers believe in the power of pre-launch to guarantee a big hit. They knew that if people heard it in advance, the excitement and anticipation would make them more eager to watch the movie. This "pre-launch" involves showing short previews, media blitz, and building campaigns on the Internet. All these are part of the strategy to ensure a commercial success.

This principle is also true for the microbusinesses. It is important to make regular communications with loyal customers and potential buyers.

How to Pre-launch?

A well-planned launch campaign gives a better result. Create a series of information campaign. The best thing to do is to tell an unfolding story.

Show a preview – Don't give too many details. Just simple heads-up that stir an interest is enough.

Why does it matter? -The vital message that you should integrate about the launch (and needs to be reinforced constantly) is why people should care.

Tell them a little about the plan -Tell some details about the launch itself – when will it happen, the possible "bonus" for early birds, and how will it work.

Getting ready- This is the calm before the storm, right before your much-awaited launch. Send a message that contains the launch details and any last-minute reminders. Your goal is to turn anticipation into decision and action.

Here it is! – The message is clear, precise and shorter. You are opening the gates and welcoming people to buy your product or service. Send a link to encourage them to take action.

Short Break

Don't rest on your laurels after the launch. A good marketer knows how to amplify the result with a little push. What happens here is equally important to what transpired on your launch.

Give an update – If something wrong happened in the launch, this is your chance to correct, address, or enhanced it. Update your customers with stories of satisfied customers.

It will soon close down – This message tells people that it is their last chance to avail the product or service with big discount, with bonus, or before your offer goes off the market.

Send a "thank you" message – This is your closing message and you are sending gratitude to everyone.

It is essential to honor your word on the launch. Stick to what you said about the launch. When you say it would end at a certain time, keep it. Even if some people are requesting exceptions, don't give in. This is how you build a reputation, an authority, and a credible business. In the long run, it will work to your advantage.

Building a Relationship

A good launch aims to convert the prospects into customers and preserve the relationship to increase the influence. Forget about people who always complain and move on. However, you *do* need to pay close attention to the broader base. Find out how they perceived your message and the value of the offer you made. Know what they said about you.

Thirty-Nine-Step Product Launch Checklist

Note: Remember that each product launch is different from the others. If you want to increase the sales significantly, follow the following steps:

THE BIG PICTURE

1. Make sure that the product or service you offer gives a clear value.

2. Decide what you will give to early buyers (rewards, bonuses, or incentives).

3. Make the launch interesting and fun for buyers and non-buyers.

4. Record a video message or video of your online launch.

5. Build anticipation.

6. Establish a real reason for urgency.

7. Publish the date and time of your launch in advance. Hit the refresh button constantly every few minutes.

8. Proofread your sales material several times. Ask someone to review them.

9. Check the Web links in your payment processor and shopping cart.

The next steps will help you make a "unique selling

proposition" or USP. It basically means that you have something that sets your offer apart from the others. *Why should be interested in what you sell?* Answer it well.

NEXT STEPS

10. Is your online product properly linked to your PayPal or shopping cart?

11. Repeatedly check the steps of the order process especially when you alter a variable.

12. Did you register the domains that are linked to your product or service?

13. Did you uploaded your files and placed in the right places?

14. Review your order page. Find errors or possible area to be improved.

15. Read your important communications like launch message, sales page, and order page aloud to check poorly-phrased statements.

16. Do you have customized graphics for your offer and affiliate partner or ads?

MONEY MATTERS

17. Set your money goal clearly. How much net income or sales do you aim for the launch?

18. Advice your bank or merchant account of incoming funds.

19. Make a backup plan for your incoming funds like a plan to switch payments to your PayPal or get another merchant account.

20. Do you have other payment options?

21. Do you have a payment plan for the high-priced product? Or maybe a discount for people who pay in full or buy bulk?

THE NIGHT BEFORE

22. Clear your email and other online tasks so your full focus is on the big launch tomorrow.

23. Create an impressive launch message to your customers, readers, and affiliates.

24. Write a blog article and other social media posts.

25. Set your alarm clock so you will be awake at least an hour before your launch.

THE BIG DAY

26. Your launch time should suit the audience. The best time is early morning East Coast time.

27. Have a soft launch 10 minutes before the actual schedule to check if all is working well.

28. Ask your first 3-5 customers if they find the order process easy to follow.

29. If it's possible, write and send a quick personal note to all buyers aside from the automated "thank you" that they receive upon purchase.

PROMOTE

This step is very important. Ask help to spread your offer. Ask your friends, acquaintances, prospects, and readers to tell their friends and families.

30. Write your affiliates to remind them of your new offer.

31. Send messages to your media contacts and journalists.

32. Post on your social networks like Facebook, Twitter, LinkedIn, and groups you are part of.

FOLLOW-UP IN ADVANCE

33. If it is necessary, you can write the first message for the follow-up series that you will be sending to your buyers.

34. Outline the additional content for your future communication and schedule it after the launch.

GOING BEYOND & ABOVE

35. How are you going to surprise your customers? Can you add some unadvertised benefits or deliverables to your product?

36. Can you do something special to say thank you to customers? (For buying extra, you call the customer or for the high-priced launch, you send a postcard)

SECOND TO LAST STEP

37. Celebrate the big day. You worked so hard for a period of time so reward yourself by buying something, have a glass of your favorite wine, or do something you like to do. You earned it.

THE FINAL STEP

38. Begin thinking and planning your next launch. Can

you build something from this project? Did you learn
anything that will help you create something better?

It is not over yet

Take a break after the launch but keep it short because the next step is important. You captured the interest of many people. Your new customers trusted you. Others who did not buy are perhaps waiting for your future products. What's your next plan?

KEY POINTS

- A good launch is like a blockbuster Hollywood movie.

- A good launch blends *tactics* (refers to "how" questions like price, pitch, and timing) with *strategy* (refers to "why" question like story, long-term plan, and plan.)

- Make a series of communication regularly before your launch.

- Tell an interesting story which considers timeliness.

- Use the Thirty-Nine-Step Product Launch Checklist as your model.

Chapter 9

Hustling: The Gentle Art of Self-Promotion

Advertising is like sex: only losers pay for it.

Hustling is about how to send your message across and made an impact. Joey Roth illustrated three 3 types of people in business- the charlatan, the martyr, and the hustler. A *charlatan* is a person who is all talk, but there is no concrete proof to back up their claims. A *martyr* is someone who is all action and has plenty of good work to back up their talk but unwilling to talk about them. A *hustler* combines talk and work.

To evolve from a charlatan to martyr to hustler, you need to do these simple steps. *First,* do something interesting and worthy to talk about. *Second,* make a list of 50 people you know and divide them into different categories – college friends, acquaintances, colleagues from an old job, etcetera). You will be asking for their assistance. *Third,* once your project is almost finished, send these people a quick note. You can make your own message. Remember that you are not sharing private information or selling something. What you are doing is letting these people know that you have something to share and you are extending an invitation for them to participate.

The next move is to consolidate hustling into your current project tasks.

What is your message?

Before you do something, think about the message that would describe your kind of business. *Why is it relevant and why is it important for people to know it now?*

Marketing Plan: The Strategic Giving

Freely give, freely receive. This is the magic ingredient of success. When you focus more on helping people and giving valuable service, you keep your business growing.

To practice strategic giving, do not take advantage of different opportunities to augment your income. Deliberately stop yourself from doing something just because of money. Do something for value- to help people. Money comes rolling in when you provide something they need to resolve their problems.

Strategize to Build Relationships

Helping people, getting to know them, and asking for help will eventually bring you real money. This strategy, however, is long-term, not a short-term tactic that quickly catapults you to success.

Say Yes First

At first, it is best to deliberately say yes to find out where the opportunity leads you. As your business grows big, you can say no and become selective. When there is an opportunity, always feel it. If it doesn't excite you, say no and move on. But if it appears meaningful and exciting, say "hell yeah" and say yes!

Give and Watch People Grab It

To engage people, offer them a giveaway or invite them to a contest. A *giveaway* is a reward that winners get while a *contest* is a sort of competition which involves judging. Between the two, the contest requires more action and engagement which generate more interest and excitement. A giveaway is easier and could generate more entries, but there is no real engagement. Experiment with both methods to gain the best benefits.

The New Future

The future is now. And just like what the statement above predicted, marketing through paid advertising has changed. Business owners and entrepreneurs utilized the power of word of mouth or hustling to promote their product or service.

The One-Page Promotion Plan

Goal: To effectively and actively recruit potential prospects to your business without being overwhelmed.

DAILY

- Keep your social media presence active by post 1-3 helpful items, touch base with people who need help, and reply to questions.
- Monitor one to two metrics only.

WEEKLY

- Seek assistance from your colleagues or ask joint promotions. Return the favor when they ask the same.
- Communicate regularly with customers and prospects

    .

AT LEAST MONTHLY

- Connect with your existing customers to know if they are okay and happy.

- Prepare a product launch, contest, or an upcoming event.

ONCE IN A WHILE

- Audit your business to find missed opportunities which can be potential projects.

- Make sure that you are working to create something significant for the business, and not reacting when things appear.

The vital point is to wake up and work on something that makes sense. Create something interesting and worthy, then spread information about it.

KEY POINTS

- Spend 50% of your business development time creating and the remaining 50% connecting with people you know, and your potential customers.

- When you build something, there is a possibility that people will come. If you do not like waiting, let them know.

- When you are still building your business, say yes to every opportunity or reasonable requests. Once you are already established, consider the "heal yeah" test and become selective.

- Follow the One-Page Promotion Plan to make sure that you are keeping a regular connecting time with people while building the other aspects of your business.

Chapter 10

Show Me the Money

Unconventional fundraising from Kickstarter to unlikely car loans

Profit is the main goal of business. Large businesses call it accountability to their shareholders. In microbusiness, you are the main shareholder and you need to protect your investment. You need recurring activities that will give you money. Without money, there is no business. So, do not be distracted by many things that call your attention.

There are two common mistakes that aspiring business owners make – thinking too much where to get capital to begin their project and thinking too little where their income will come from. If you want to avoid them or fix them, a simple solution is necessary – if possible, spend little at the start, then make more money.

Part I –Start Low

There are two essential principles that business must focus on

—creating money and profit. Borrowing is completely optional. Why risk debt if you are not very sure about the success of your project. It is possible, to begin with, a low budget.

1. *Michael Trainer* built a media production company with $2,500 investment to buy a camera.

2. Cherry Vitry began her tour guide business for food lovers in Denver with a startup cost of $28.

3. Chris Dunphy and Cheri Ve Ard established a health-care software consultancy called Technomadia for $125.

Source Funds

When you need money to finance business, the best alternative is to get from your savings. If your saving is not enough or you do not want to risk your egg nest, try "crowd raising" through <u>Kickstarter.com</u>.

Part II- Create Money & More Profits

These 3 principles that helped many business owners earn more profits are:

1. *Price the product or service based on its benefit not on the cost of production*

Be ready to stand your ground when you based your price on the benefits of your offer. Some people will complain about your pricing but don't waver. You know the real value of your product or service.

2. *Offer your customers a limited range of prices*

To ensure optimum profitability, offer more than one price. This increases your income even without increasing the number of customers.

3. *Get paid for the same offer more than once*

This final strategy is about making sure that your launch is successful to bring repeated sales from loyal customers. Think about subscriptions, membership site, or continuity program.

More than the Money

Aside from the money, you have more than you think. You have access to all types of social and financial capital which you can use if necessary. People trust you because of the help you provided. Most of them will not think twice to lend their assistance when you need it. Keep building your authority and trustworthiness.

KEY POINTS

- The main goal of operating a business is to create money.

- Every day, many people start and operate a successful business without borrowing or enlisting outside investment.

- Get paid more than once using different strategies to increase the odds of success.

- Be creative to access help, money, or anything you need.

PART III

LEVERAGE AND NEXT STEPS

Chapter 11

Moving On Up

Tweaking your way to the bank: How small actions create big increases in income.

There are several factors that can help you move up and earn more money from your existing business. The first one is momentum. Next is constant attention. And, third is a series of small regular and consistent actions (tweaks).

Tweaks are small changes which bring big impact. They are the not-so-secret methods to improve income. Here are some examples of tweaks:

- *Increase your website traffic*

- *Convert your visitors into customers*

- *Increase your price*

- *Offer more*

TAKE ACTION

Build your own "Hall of Fame" – Ask your best customers to share their stories on how your product or service helps them.

Get referrals – ask specific help from your customer to spread your offer.

Create upsell - It is the most powerful tactic and the easiest to increase your sales income

Start a contest - Create a bigger audience for your next offer by giving away a prize.

Give the best guarantee – Offer a no pain the ass money-back guarantee like 110% assurance by taking care of the delivery.

Product to Service, Service to Product

Another simple way to add a revenue source is to create a product from service-based business or a service from a product-based business.

Think of a new version of your product like coaching, consulting, teaching, technical support, or "jumpstart sessions" services. And for your service offer, create a "productized" version of it.

Raise Prices Regularly

Do not be afraid to raise the price of your product or service. Customers will pay for the real value of your offer. A slight increase will not make them leave you suddenly.

The Best Social Media Strategy:

Talk About Yourself

If you don't know what to share online, start by talking about you and your business. Talk about what you are doing and what is happening in the place where you are in. Do something interesting, then, write and post the story on your site.

A Note of Caution

Scale your business the way you want to. If you deliberately choose to remain small, stick to it. You can grow your business in 2 ways: vertically (by creating different levels of engagement with your customers and going deep) or horizontally (by creating various products and going wide).

KEY POINTS

- Increasing income by "moving on up" is much easier.
- Oftentimes, you grow your business by making careful choices.
- Employ creative series of cross-sells and upsells, add a product to a service-based business (or vice versa),

or do other tweaks.

- Expand vertically expand horizontally.

Chapter 12

How to Franchise Yourself

Instructions on cloning yourself for fun and profit

Buying a business franchise is considered a bad idea because, in reality, you bought a job for yourself and your employees. You operate and manage it precisely in the way they tell you to, no exceptions, and no deviations. From hiring to the color of uniform you should wear in "your business." If this business fails, it will be taken back from you and they will resell it to another buyer.

So, why buy one when you can build a real business which you can call your own.

Grow Your Business

One of the ways to grow a business is through leverage. It is about taking your passion, skills, and activities to a higher level to gain excellent returns. When you create your own business, you can be strategic. Self-made franchising allows you to reach different types of audience – the core group and a related group. It gives you two options- Reach more people with the same offer or reach different people with a new offer.

The best example of the first option is a *"hub-and-spoke"* model. The *hub* is the primary website which is usually an e-commerce site which is also a place to build a community forum, a blog, or anything creative. It is where you drive traffics, prospects, and customers. The *spokes* (also called outposts) are the places where you regularly spend time. They include the social media sites, your blog or others blogs comment sections, networking events, or actual meetings. The goal of every spoke (outpost) is to support the hub's works.

Partnership

Owner of an international professional services company in Stuttgart, Germany, Ralf Hilderbrandt explained the concept of $1 + 1 = 3$. He said that a successful collaboration or partnership should be 33% larger than the sum of individual's own accomplishments. A true partnership creates more than a separate list of tasks.

A joint venture with someone you trust is one path of self-franchising.

One-Page Partnership Agreement

A simple written agreement is enough. The most important factors are trust and strong relationship.

KEY POINTS

- Leverage contacts and skills through partnerships, affiliate recruitment, and outsourcing to operate your business in different places.
- Utilize the hub-and-spoke business model.
- A good partnership creates better leverage. Simplify your arrangements by using the One-Page Partnership Agreement.
- Decide carefully if outsourcing is for you.

Chapter 13

Going Long

Become as big as you want to be (and no bigger).

You learned from the stories in this book that not all entrepreneurs are risk-takers, they just define security and risk differently.

The Choices

Every successful owner of a business will eventually face a choice – whether accidental or otherwise.

Option 1: Stay Small

Option 2: Go Medium

Option 3: Split the Difference

Create and Work on your Business

When your project grows big and bigger, you will find yourself spending most of your time taking care and responding to almost everything. You left little time to creating something. Stop putting out fires. Focus your time working *on* the business.

Set 45 minutes every morning without the Internet. Use this time to do activities that will grow your business. Think about the *forward motion.*

- *Develop your business* – It is the work that can grow your business. Do you have new products or services that you can offer? Are you pursuing joint ventures or new partnership?

- *Develop new offers* – It involves utilizing the existing resources to create a new offer, a launch event, or a sale to generate attention and profit.

- *Fix long-standing issues*- Instead of addressing the problems directly or ignoring the perpetual issues, you can utilize your non-firefighting time to deal with the root cause.

What about Health Insurance?

One big question that many aspiring entrepreneurs face is insurance. Once they leave their regular day jobs and begin a business, they become self-employed. Here are some options for you:

- *Buy a high-deductible policy and pay cash for visits to the doctor* – A high-deductible policy covers accidents and serious illnesses. Save your own health fund.

- *Get insured through your partner* – Many entrepreneurs relied on their spouse or partner's insurance coverage while building their business.

- *Join a concierge program* – For paying $150-300 as monthly, you can avail of doctor's care for preventive need and primary diseases.

- *Self-insure or use an HSA* – Others choose to take extra care to avoid being sick.

- *Stay on COBRA as long as possible* – COBRA allows you to receive health coverage for a period of time and pay the same amount you used to when you are still employed.

Communicate with customers

Initiate communication through updates, newsletters, emails, and inquiries. Spend 45 minutes daily to do it.

Review Prices

A regular review of your prices helps you determine if it is necessary to make an increase.

Monitor Your Business

Your main concern is to grow your business. Here are two-pronged strategies you can use to do it:

Step 1: Choose 1-2 metrics and pay attention to them. Check sales, incoming leads, and cash flow.

Step 2: Review other concerns weekly and check the overall status of your business every month.

Do not delegate all financial matters to someone. You should have an upper knowledge about it.

Here are some metrics you should track:

Sales per day: How much is your daily income?

Visitors or leads per day: How many people visit your site or sign-up to get more information?

Sales conversion rate: What percentage of leads or visitors become your customers?

Average order price: How much your customers spend when they place an order?

Net promoter score: How many of your customers will refer the business to their friends or family?

Build to Sell It

John Warrillow was the owner of 4 companies who retired after selling them. He opted to become a writer, speaker, and an investor. He is now advocating a business model for entrepreneurs who aim to sell their businesses someday.

BUILT TO SELL—$100 STARTUP COMPARISON

Startup	Built to Sell	$100
Required Capital	Variable but usually high	Variable but usually low
Employees	Required	Optional
Freedom Payoff	Big payday	No big payday
Secondary Benefit	Build & move on	Do what you love

John's business model is about creating a business that is distinctly apart from the owner's skills and selling it for a profit. The $100 Startup is about creating a business that is intrinsically linked to the owner's passion or skills.

KEY POINTS

- There are many roads to freedom, find yours by combining different working arrangements.

- You can "go long" by choosing to remain small or pursuing growth.

- Work "on" by devoting a period of time to do activities that are related to business improvement.

- Monitor 1-2 key metrics daily. The others should be reviewed weekly, bi-monthly or monthly.

- If you aim to sell the business one day, build teams and decrease owner's dependency.

Chapter 14

But What If I Fail?

How to succeed even if your roof caves in on you?

All success stories have phases of failures, disappointments, loss of motivation, hopeless, and other emotional episodes that almost make the business owners quit.

John T. Unger

John is a sculpture artist from Michigan. According to him, *the third best thing* that happened to his life was when his studio's roof collapsed while he was standing on it and shoveling snow. The building was totally destroyed. He continued working despite the winter cold. He warmed himself with unvented kerosene heater which is considered illegal. It was a bleak scenario, but it suddenly changed when the bank assessed the damage and gave him a check worth $10,000. John used the commission to pay the down payments of 2 buildings he wanted to buy. The second-best thing was when he lost his job as graphic designer in 2000, during the period of dot-com crash. He lost everything after that- his income, his apartment, his girlfriend, and a piece of thumb while moving out from the apartment. He was depressed. His friends told him to move on and find another job. John knew that it wasn't easy in Michigan. He decided to continue working on his project and goal. And the first best thing happened during one late night. John was held hostage with a gun to his head for 10 seconds by a crazed cab driver after a disagreement. He managed to escape and was lucky to be alive.

Unsolicited Advice & Asking Permission

Advice is very different from permission. If you want to pursue your dreams and goals, go for them. You don't need other people's permission. Stop waiting and begin your $100 startup now. If you know what you are doing, simply do it. Stop waiting. Act on it.

Fear Not

All business owners including those earning $50,000 or move every year have fears, concerns, and worries. After asking many of them, Chris arrived in two broad concerns- external and internal.

External concerns are associated with money and changing marketplace. Many worry about other people copying or stealing their unique and original works. Employers with hired employees worry about payroll and cash flow.

Internal concerns are related to the need to "fake it" or keep the wheels rolling after their initial passion or motivation faded away. Worries and fears are usually linked to identity issues.

The $100 Recap

Before concluding this book, Chris recapped the key lessons that are incorporated into different stories.

The journey to personal freedom lies directly in giving value to others.

Borrowing money to start your business is optional. Many business owners start their own microbusiness with $100 or less.

Focus on the convergence point – between your passion and what product or service you can offer to people who are willing to pay for it.

Always remember that if you are good at one thing, most probably, you are pretty goods at something else. Always find out what people want, then, find ways to deliver it to them.

There is no formal consulting school. So, set up yours and charge rate for specialized consulting service.

Some business models use a little budget. Find out how you can contribute to the knowledge economy.

Follow the One-Page Business plan or any quick-start guides and act on your dream. Action always beats planning.

To generate better and greater results, craft an attractive offer, use the art of hustling, and create a launch event.

Find your way to earn your first $1.26 sale as soon as possible. Then, keep improving. Ignore the things that are not working or helping you.

Franchise yourself through outsourcing, creating different venture, or partnering with someone you trust.

Decide what type of business you want to build.

It's only when you go along that you get things better.

Finally, always find lessons in failures. You'll probably encounter one or two false starts while on the road to personal freedom.

Be ready to create your own fortune and live life with freedom.

KEY POINTS

- Advice can help you, but most of the time, all you need is to step out and make a big leap. Do not ask permission from other people.

- The biggest battle is internal- your fears and inertia. It is more challenging than external factors.

- When you experience the "moment you knew" or success story, hold on to it because the experiences will empower you and aid you when life gets tough.

- And remember the most important lesson of this book – Stop wasting precious time living the life of another.

Conclusion

You have come to the end of this book. You learned the significant lessons and essential secrets of many successful business owners who followed their passions. They created and contributed something to the world by giving value, and they gained two things- financial independence and personal freedom.

To recap what this book is all about- *Chapter 1* taught you how passion or hobby can be turned into a profitable business. *Chapter 2* reminded you to always give what people want. *Chapter 3* helped you create a business out of passion. *Chapter 4* provided an inspiration to consider a life where you can work anywhere in the world. *Chapter 5* gave you ways to understand your customers better. *Chapter 6* taught you how to make a sound one-page business plan. *Chapter 7* helped you create a good offer that attracted people to pay for it. *Chapter 8* taught you why you need a good launch. *Chapter 9* showed you how to use the art of hustling to promote your business. *Chapter 10* taught you ways to find startup money and why borrowing is not an option. *Chapter 11* gave you reliable tweaks to bring in the money. *Chapter 12* showed you ways to clone yourself and do business in different places. *Chapter 13* gave you reasons why choosing to stay small can help you grow the business. *Chapter 14* gave you stories why failure is overrated.

Finally, remind yourself of Chris statement- *"Work to improve your own circumstances, with freedom as the goal and value as the currency."*

You will soon arrive at your privileged destination.

Final Thoughts

Hey! Did you enjoy this book? We sincerely hope you thoroughly enjoyed this short read and have gotten immensely valuable insights that will help you in any areas of your life.

Would it be too greedy if we ask for a review from you?

It takes 1 minute to leave 1 review to possibly influence 1 more person's decision to read just 1 book which may change their 1 life. Your 1 minute matters and we value it and thank you so much for giving us your 1 minute. If it sucks, just say it sucks. Period.

FREE BONUS

P.S. Is it okay if we overdeliver?

Here at Abbey Beathan Publishing, we believe in overdelivering way beyond our reader's expectations. Is it okay if we overdeliver?

Here's the deal, we're going to give you an extremely valuable cheatsheet of "Accelerated Learning". We've partnered up with Ikigai Publishing to present to you the exclusive bonus of "Accelerated Learning Cheatsheet"

What's the catch? We need to trust you… You see, we want to overdeliver and in order for us to do that, we've to trust our reader to keep this bonus a secret to themselves. Why? Because we don't want people to be getting our exclusive accelerated learning cheatsheet without even buying our books itself. Unethical, right?

Ok. Are you ready?

Simply Visit this link: http://bit.ly/acceleratedcheatsheet

We hope you'll enjoy our free bonuses as much as we've enjoyed preparing it for you!

Free Bonus #2: Free Book Preview of Summary:
Unf*ck Yourself
The Book at a Glance

Gary John Bishop's *Unf*ck Yourself: Get Out of Your Head and Into Your Life* is unlike most self-help books in that it is written in a straightforward, no-frills, even sometimes crass kind of language. But the title already clues the reader in on that.

Within this book, you will find Bishop's seven personal assertions (which are also the title of each chapter). They are intended to dismantle the negative self-talk that you consciously or unconsciously engage in throughout everyday life. By self-talk, he means the kinds of automatic conversations and thoughts that you have with yourself which are often negative and self-defeating. Through the assertions Bishop means to give readers a "conversational slap from the universe" to help seize their true potential and live out their best life.

The first chapter introduces the concept of self-talk and details how language shapes thoughts and ultimately changes lives. Drawing upon psychological and phenomenological thinkers like Albert Ellis, Ludwig Wittgenstein and Martin Heidegger, Bishop stresses how shifting the way you think and talk about your experiences will change how you feel about them.

Chapter 2 opens with the statement that you have the life you are willing to put up with. Here the mantra is to stop the blame game. No matter the circumstances happening in your life that seem out of control, you decide how you act in the presence and aftermath of those events. The chapter lingers heavily on willingness and the creation of a state of purpose in which you stop blaming other people or circumstances for things that happen to you, and instead start personally asserting your power to re-frame your situation.

The third chapter delves into how the brain is wired to win. The thing with the brain, however, is that most of its functions are unconscious or automated. That means that the brain will follow a set path regardless of whether that path coincides with what you consciously claim you want to do, become or accomplish. If you've thought of yourself in particular ways -- which means that you've wired your brain to work in a particular way -- you might in fact be setting your own limits from success.

Chapter 4 — *I got this* — is all about putting problems into proper perspective. Here, Bishop details how small problems can turn into huge ones, and how you may in fact be creating problems where there are none. In those moments, he advises looking back on your past experiences, re-contextualizing the present and finding grace in those moments. And you can also take that exercise into the future to see how you might deal with things yet to come.

The next chapter deals with certainty, uncertainty, risks and potential. Setting his statements against the evolutionary backdrop of the human brain's aversion to risks in the face of a then much scarier, more dangerous world, Bishop raises the point that the uncertain is where new things happen. Staying within the bounds of what is known means depriving the self of the potentials in life.

In Chapter 6 you get to the thesis statement of this book: you are not your thoughts; you are what you do. Having goals that are actionable will propel you forward. Negative, damaging or diminishing thoughts will hold you back. Bishop talks about motivation and how *doing* changes *thinking*.

Relentlessness is the highlight of the seventh chapter. Following up on Chapter 6 — where the reader is moved towards action — , Chapter 7 now doubles down on relentlessness, that quality of not giving up long after motivation or evidence of success seems to have gone. It is about determined and focused actions that you take again and again, time after time.

Chapter 8 opens with the old adage: expect the unexpected. With an anecdote, Bishop details how a well-meaning goal can turn into a disaster because it has been bogged down by expectations. When you think of life in terms of how you want and expect it to be, you give yourself no favors. Instead, be present, see life for how it is, and learn to adapt.

Finally, Chapter 9 brings all the points together into the subtitle for the book, getting out your head and into your life. In another way, act in the external world in order to improve your internal one.

Within this book, you just might find the thing that makes you get up and change your life.

1 – In the beginning…

You are caught in a loop of negative thoughts. There's a voice inside your head that insists that you are lazy or stupid. That you'll never get the career you dream of or find a lasting relationship. Or that you'll never lose weight. Or find any happiness.

That voice is the negative self-talk that you have harbored for life without even meaning to. It's a destructive stream of thought that hinders you from unlocking your potential and actually achieving your dreams.

And the impact of negative self-talk is backed by scientific research. According to experiments conducted by Professor Will Hart of the University of Alabama, people who described a negative event tended to also feel more negatively. The language they used to recall experiences influenced how they felt. Similarly, the language that you use when you think of your circumstances also dictates how you deal with them.

Thankfully, the opposite is also true. Positive self-talk can lead to a positive outlook as well. It can improve mood, increase productivity, and give confidence.

The Difference Between Success and Failure

The way you think and talk influences your life. Imagine some scenario in the past where you had the thought that everything was going wrong, or that that would be the end of your life. You definitely weren't being very rational. That kind of negative self-talk can lead to frustration, anger or sadness.

Your self-talk can be self-fulfilling. The more you tell yourself that something is too hard or impossible to achieve, the more difficult it would be for you to accomplish that thing. Therefore, you may be talking yourself out of doing the things your rational mind may want you to do.

How Language Changes Our Lives

You must be careful of your perceptions and how they cause you to think negatively. Because the language you use in thought tend to be internalized, changing your patterns of behavior along with it.

A person who views life negatively will tend to act in accordance to that worldview. Perhaps he will put in less effort, or go into tasks expecting them not to amount to anything. The worldview will become that person's reality. Conversely, someone else with a positive perception of the world may be driven to work even harder. They will be energized and determined. They will create the world where success is always just around the corner.

You have the power to hold yourself down or lift yourself up. You can create the reality you want within your own mind by being conscious of how you perceive circumstances that happen to you.

Re-train Your Brain – One Word at a Time

Neuroplasticity, the phenomenon in the brain wherein physical structures are actually shaped by thoughts, is something that can be exploited. You just have to take charge through conscious, decisive and assertive self-talk. Make the choice to talk in a helpful way instead of a harmful way.

Re-train the brain to think in a manner that re-shapes your reality. Re-frame problems and turn them instead into new opportunities. Become engaged by life rather than frustrated by it.

Assertive vs. Narrative

You can assert your power by doing away with talking about who you *will* be, or what you're *going* to do, and instead claim the moment of the here and now. Use statements like "I am…" or "I accept…" The narrative of the "I will…" gives you an out. It describes what's to come instead of what is in the present.

When you say you will, what happens when you suddenly encounter temptations like fast food, or a sale? Your enthusiasm in the beginning of a task or a project can peter out and then you'll fall back into your old, unconscious behavioral patterns. Speaking assertively in life allows you to actively intervene in the moment and not just be fired up in the beginning only to lose steam as you go along.

Using This Book

Reading along will help you to understand the power of self-talk. You'll realize the many ways in which language and internal conversations can change the way you behave and act.

Use a highlighter or flags and mark up the passages or sections that ring very true to you. You can dip in and out of chapters. Even if they're written as a series, you can take lessons from each one. They stand on their own.

When you're stuck, or see yourself falling into unconscious self-talk again, return to your favorite sections and find the words that can make a difference in your life.

SUMMARY:

The 33 Strategies of War

ABBEY BEATHAN

Legal & Disclaimer

The information contained in this book is not designed to replace or take the place of any form of medicine or professional medical advice. The information in this book has been provided for educational and entertainment purposes only.

The information contained in this book has been compiled from sources deemed reliable, and it is accurate to the best of the Author's knowledge; however, the Author cannot guarantee its accuracy and validity and cannot be held liable for any errors or omissions. Changes are periodically made to this book. You must consult your doctor or get professional medical advice before using any of the suggested remedies, techniques, or information in this book. Images used in this book are not the same as of that of the actual book. This is a totally separate and different entity from that of the original book titled: "*The 33 Strategies of War*"

Upon using the information contained in this book, you agree to hold harmless the Author from and against any damages, costs, and expenses, including any legal fees potentially resulting from the application of any of the information provided by this guide. This disclaimer applies to any

Table of Contents

The Book at a Glance

The 33 Strategies of War is a 2006 non-fiction book written by widely-praised American author, Robert Greene. He describes this as the "guide to the subtle social game of everyday life informed by the... military principles of war". This book is comprised of discussions and cases on hostile and protective methodologies form a wide assortment of individuals and conditions citing examples from Tet Offensive, Lawrence of Arabia, Alexander the Great and French statesman and military leader, Napoleon Bonaparte.

Published by Penguin Group, this non-fiction novel is compartmentally partitioned into five sections: Self-Directed Warfare, Organizational (Team) Warfare, Defensive Warfare, Offensive Warfare and Unconventional (Dirty) Warfare. Greene wonderfully clarifies each area by bestowing various methodologies, a couple of portrayal of fights, political and business circumstances and his elucidation of every situation. The author ends each chapter with what he calls a "Reversal"- a concise exchange of where the procedure may not have any significant bearing, an opposite view or protection from the strategies he has written.

Robert Greene was born to Jewish parents and was raised in Los Angeles, California. He graduated at University of

Wisconsin in Madison, and has travelled to many different places and has lived in London, Paris, and Barcelona; he speaks several languages and has worked as a translator. He currently lives in Los Angeles. He has worked in New York as an editor and writer at several magazines, including Esquire, and in Hollywood as a story developer and writer. He has authored best-selling books *The 48 Laws of Power*, *Mastery, The Art of Seduction, The 33 Strategies of War, The 50th Law* and *The Laws of Human Nature* and has been widely mentioned by rappers and big personalities alike. Known for his writing style of power, strategy and seduction, Greene is a widely praised author that has made a household name of his impeccable talent.

PART I:

SELF DIRECTED WARFARE

Greene opens *The 33 Strategies of War* by characterizing the fundamental character of war. Portrayed by Merriam and Webster, he describes war as a conflict carried on by energy of arms, as between nations or between parties inside a nation; battling, as through land, sea, or air. The author then infuses that for each war to be won; a methodology must be painstakingly arranged and that everything begins with what individuals put in their minds. He adds that for a person to wind up as a genuine strategist, this individual should make three strides consisting of first, progress toward becoming mindful of the shortcoming and ailment that can grab hold of the psyche, twisting its vital forces; secondly, Greene says that a person should pronounce a sort of war on their self to make them advance; thirdly, Greene advises to wage merciless, constant fight on the foes inside a person by applying certain techniques.

He explains that the book's next four chapters was designed to make the reader mindful of the clutters that are most likely prospering in a person's mind at any moment and to arm a person with certain methodologies.

1. Declare War on Your Enemies:

The Polarity Strategy

In the first chapter of *The 33 Strategies of War* entitled "Declare War on Your Enemies", Greene narrates a story of how in 401 BC Xenophon drove Greek soldiers of fortune into the Persian region. Procured to battle, Xenophon needed to transform a soldier of fortune band of Greeks into a brought together gathering battling for self-conservation. They needed to distinguish the adversary, decide the explanations behind their battle and fight their own issues. At the point when their pioneer kicked the bucket and they didn't have anything more to battle for, encompassed by the adversary, they needed to wind up a concentrated power battling their way back home. The warriors' soul was squashed - they had powerless assurance and began battling one another. Xenophon joined them, consequently vanquishing the internal foe. Concentrating on survival, the possibility of returning home alive to family and companions influenced them to continue on.

The main idea of the first chapter is that, you can't swing a sword without realizing what to hit with it. It's you against

106

the world and it's you against yourself. You can't battle successfully unless you can recognize them. Figure out how to smoke them out, at that point deep down announce war. Your adversaries can fill you with reason and bearing. To battle you should know and distinguish your rivals. Battle your internal devils. Try not to let your psyche, your feelings and your sense of self control you. Know yourself and outer adversaries won't have the capacity to hurt you.

Greene quotes the strong icon, Margaret Thatcher, and narrates how she characterized her battle and her rival. She battled constantly for what she felt was correct not calling it quits despite resistance driving her assignments to consummation.

As for the initial chapter's "Reversal", Greene outlines what he says should be key points and identifies them as:

- Characterize your rival.

- If all else fails, test to guarantee he is your adversary.

- Having rivals infers your significance, keep up your core interest.

- Utilize your rivals to occupy consideration from you.

2. Do Not Fight the Last War:

The Guerilla-War-Of-The-Mind Strategy

In the second chapter of *The 33 Strategies of War* entitled "Do Not Fight the Last War", Greene tells the story of Miyamoto Musashi, one of history's most hazardous Samurais. In this chapter, Greene tells the readers a story of how Musashi used to switch up his battling design, changing his strategies consistently to keep his rivals speculating and on edge. The anxiety and suspicion this incurred on his adversaries made them simple targets, concluding that what has worked before, may not work once more. Therefore, Greene advises to disregard the past and adjust to current circumstances, consistently evolving, regularly developing. He further quotes George Bernard Shaw who said "The main man I know who carries on sensibly is my tailor; he takes as much time as is needed he sees me. The lay go ahead with their old estimations and anticipate that me will fit them."

Greene strongly suggests that people should try not to *Fight the Last War* or also called the Guerrilla-War-of-the-Mind Strategy. He expresses that tactics age, therefore, one should keep strategies crisp and dependably grow new ones.

Greene injects the story of "The Last War" where in 1806

108

Prince Friedrich Ludwig of Hohenlohe-Ingelfingen battled Napoleon; however his procedures were those of Frederick the Great and were old and tired. Napoleon's inventive methodologies outmaneuvered him. On the other side of the fence, which Greene calls "The Present War", Miyamoto Musashi, a samurai, had a peculiar arrangement of characterizing duels and would build up an example for his battling, however would frequently change his strategies to perplex and confound his adversaries. Musashi, as Greene says, is persistent to adjust his strategies managed his rivals no solace.

For the second chapters' "Reversal", Greene advises his readers to:

- Drop assumptions.

- Disregard the last war.

- Reevaluate convictions and standards.

- Continue designing new plans.

- Adjust to current circumstances.

- Turn around course doing the opposite has been done previously.

3. Amidst The Turmoil of Events, Do Not Lose Your Presence of Mind:

The Counterbalance Strategy

In the third chapter of *The 33 Strategies of War* entitled "Amidst the Turmoil of Events, Do Not Lose Your Presence of Mind", Greene portrays the story of Master Nelson who resisted his insane authority in the fight at Copenhagen in 1801, keeping a quiet head in a most frenzied circumstance. Greene considers Nelson's behavior as a *Hyper-Aggressive Tactic*. Nelson blatantly ignored his administrator's power and seeing the front line for what it was, crushed the Danish naval force. The lesson for this chapter is that you need to remain on watch, because as Greene says, every other person is in mayhem. Try not to be threatened by tumult; try not to freeze and make sure you search out the contention responding quickly, when the open door presents itself. Ensure that you remain centered, characterize your objectives and have the certainty to accomplish those objectives. With this set up, endeavor toward that objective constantly.

In another scenario, Greene gives an example of a *Confined Buddha Tactic* in movie executive Alfred Hitchcock who dependably had an entire comprehension and plan for his motion pictures. Hitchcock knew the look and feel that he

110

needed to accomplish so he designed his precise approach, however befuddling to others, and this gave him a quiet disposition on the set.

As for the "Reversal" of this third chapter, Green advises the following:

- Try not to get disappointed by individuals less key or absurd, utilize them further bolstering your good fortune.

- Search out the contention, don't avoid it.

- Keep up good judgment; don't give yourself a chance to be scared without anyone else's input or others.

- Try not to freeze, center around what you are certain about.

- Build up a fast response sense, decide.

- Depend just on yourself, limit dependence on others.

4. Create a Sense of Urgency and Desperation: *The Death-Ground Strategy*

In the fourth chapter of *The 33 Strategies of War* entitled "Create a Sense of Urgency and Desperation", Greene opens the section by telling the story of Fyodor Dostoevsky and how he was able to tell that his days were numbered. Dostoevsky confronted his execution and made utilization of his chance by making every one of his fills in as though they were his last, since they exceptionally well could've been. The private involvement with his mortality enabled him to transcend life's details.

Greene considers this as an example of making sense of urgency and desperation through a death ground strategy. He advises that when there are no different alternatives, people battle harder because on the off chance that the decision is crucial they don't have anything to lose.

He also tells the story of Spanish conquistador Hernán Cortés, who in 1504 utilized this strategy as he expelled the capacity of his 500 men to come back to Cuba. They needed to battle the Aztecs despite the fact that terribly out numbered. Cortés begun by setting sail to the New World at 19 years old and later joined an undertaking to Cuba. In 1518, he set off to investigate Mexico. He deliberately adjusted some local people groups against others to topple them. Lord Charles I selected him legislative leader of New Spain in 1522. He is famously known for defeating the Aztec empire and claiming the country Mexico for his motherland, Spain.

Like these stories, Greene tells his readers that when you encounter passing, you dispense with life's superfluous items with the tendency of implanting defeat details people absurdly think of, consistently ending their lives. Greene states that Dostoevsky's work is excellent; in light of the fact that he was anxious he also didn't look for comfort. A person can't sit tight for the correct time and is never completely arranged to begin. "Tu fui sense of self eris." Greene says, or in English, "*As you are, I was. As I am, you will be*".

For the "Reversal", Greene lists the following:

- Take the unparalleled risk approach.

- Try not to hold up to be prepared, act sooner.

- Go about as though it is you against the world.

- Remain anxious, don't look for comfort.

PART II:

ORGANIZATIONAL (TEAM) WARFARE

For the second part of *The 33 Strategies of War*, Greene implies that for a leader to be able to achieve true success, he must know how to effectively manage his people. Basically, the general population that you encircle yourself with will impact your mentality. With regards to contributing, it's critical to encircle yourself with a win group that will help make your objectives a reality.

Understand also that the general population you encircle yourself with, will be an impression of your identity. Think about various gatherings of individuals and see where you fit in. Finding the opportune individuals will make it less demanding to take part in significant discussion and to capitalize on the advantages of being a piece of a win group. Greene suggests that it is best to incorporate speed and portability with the exact structure of your armed force. That implies having a solitary expert to finish everything, staying away from the reluctance and perplexity of isolated authority. It implies giving officers a feeling of the general objective to be refined and the scope to make a move to meet that objective; rather than responding like machines, they can react to occasions in the field. Finally, it implies spurring fighters, making a general esprit de corps that gives them overwhelming energy. With powers composed in this way, a general can adjust to conditions speedier than the adversary can, picking up a chosen advantage.

5. Avoid the Snares of Groupthink:

The Command-And-Control Strategy

To start the second part of the book, *The 33 Strategies of War* and the fifth chapter entitled "Avoid the Snares of Groupthink", Greene carefully narrates the story of General George Marshall who built up an arrangement of protégés deliberately showing them his logic of charge, as they held similar convictions and ran their situations as indicated by his vision. This made the capacity for him to know and put stock in the activities of his subordinates. The General showed his rationalities on initiative to a modest bunch of protégés he'd put into definitive positions with high hazard obligations. Familiarly, one of these men was Dwight Eisenhower. The General strategically places commanders of outrageous specialists, knowing the circumstance would be keep running as indicated by his convictions and style.

Greene says that an example of "The Broken Chain" is when in the early World War I, the British assaulted Constantinople endeavoring to open access to the Black Sea to supply Russia and to encourage assaulting the Germans from the East. General Ian Hamilton drove his summon by assigning subtle elements to subordinates and this brought about absence of comprehension of the strategic goals of securing Tekke Tepe,

116

consequently losing the fight.

The lesson of this chapter is that you need levels of leadership you can depend on. You are the General, the leader and the boss however; you can't have your head all over and oversee everything that is going in the place of operations. The best thing to do, as per Greene's advice is to set up remote frameworks and faithful pioneers that will ensure the coveted result and will act in your behalf, similarly having the same end goal as you. Utilize this people to adjust your shortcomings with their qualities and guarantee they generally stay up with the latest. Regardless, be mindful so as not to surrender excessively of your own power and use. Take order and control and try not to be excessively tyrant and not very frail.

The "Reversal" for this chapter is:

- Be like a "Remote Control"

- Make a hierarchy of leadership

- Search for individuals to fill your voids of information, depend on them yet don't end up hostage to them

- Separated administration is unsafe

- Guarantee you get quick data from the trenches

117

- Be careful about the politically disposed in your middle

6. Segment Your Forces:

The Controlled-Chaos Strategy

The sixth chapter of the book *The 33 Strategies of War* entitled "Segment Your Forces" starts with Greene's narration of how Napoleon Bonaparte confronted an assault by Austrian troops in 1805 whereupon Napoleon separated his troops and sent them into fight with particular directions of encompassing the adversary. The French units were allowed to move, adaptable and snappy and the Austrian troops surrendered.

This is a perfect example of a "Computed Disorder", as Greene calls it. This is the inverse of Concentrating Your Forces; subsequently it's on you to know, when to join together and when to separate your armed force. Make sure to be moderate, however solid or quick and exact. Greene instills that the basic components in war are speed and flexibility - the capacity to move and settle on choices speedier than the foe. You always have to be five steps ahead of them – the more, the better. He says it is best to break your powers into autonomous gatherings that can work alone and give them the soul of the crusade, a mission to achieve, and space to run.

Greene concludes in this chapter that littler units are more dexterous, versatile and deft and lists the key warfare points as:

- Keep yourself in a place of power

- Impart the theory of following charges "in soul" not "by the letter"

- Make animosity in the troops with the goal that when they are separated they take after a similar logic

7. Transform Your War into a Crusade:
Morale Strategies

Greene opens the seventh chapter of *The 33 Strategies of War* entitled "Transform Your War into a Crusade" by giving a few examples of people who famously managed their men well. He tells several stories including the stories of Oliver Cromwell, who had minimal British military foundation, joined the military to lead a campaign of the Puritans. He enrolled similar people and instructed a considerable unit. In the same behavior, Lyndon Johnson kept his groups buckling down by keeping acclaim illusive and encouraging rivalry to get that acclaim in 1931. In the year 1950, North American football's Green Bay Packers procured Vince Lombardi who treated all players similarly and influenced them all to win regard and acclaim. He utilized the dread of open criticize to keep colleagues in line. In addition, in the year 1796: Napoleon stimulated his troops with the "Soul of the Republic" for their fights, frequently going by troops or injured so they would see his vitality and assemble their spirit. His story also focused largely on how Hannibal masterminded a focused war recreation to exhibit how far his men would go to join the up and coming battle, to indicate what they were made of.

121

Greene analyzes that this is an example of an exercise in authority. Overseeing men well means showing others how it's done and you utilize the impacts of feeling by underscoring that you are battling for a respectable aim and that "God is your ally." It's about the group, its soul, the aggregate vitality and the accomplishment of the mission ahead. You rebuff and reward conduct as needs be. Influence them to see their survival is attached to the achievement of the armed force all in all. You bond together through each activity and dispose of the odd one out, who disturb your initiative. Inspire them to contemplate themselves and more about the gathering. Include them in a reason, a campaign against an abhorred adversary.

Greene calls this "The Art of Man Management" and lists his "Reversals" as the following:

- Be a pioneer

- Battle for a reason

- Accommodate the group

- Show others how it's done

- Center the group's vitality

- Dodge inertness

- Nourish the feelings to bolster the reason

- Remunerate and rebuff sparingly

- However let the group know they exist

- Manufacture group history and utilize it to security

- Expel the alienated

- Lastly, make a climate of battling for something honorable—a reason or a need

PART III:

DEFENSIVE WARFARE

For the second part of *The 33 Strategies of War*, Greene explains defensive warfare. He tells his readers that if a person chooses to battle in a guarded way, it certainly isn't an indication of shortcoming; rather, it is the stature of vital knowledge, and may be considered as an effective style of taking up arms. In fact, the prerequisites are straightforward which may consist of taking advantage of assets, battling with the consummate economy and connecting with just in fights that are essential. In addition, a person should know how and when to withdraw, attracting a forceful foe into an unwise assault. At that point, sitting tight quietly for his snapshot of depletion, dispatch an awful counterattack.

The chapters of the second part of the book will give examples on the basic examples of defensive warfare like knowing the economy of means, counterattack, terrorizing and discouragement, and how to withdraw skillfully and hide when under forceful assault.

8. Pick Your Battles Carefully:

The Perfect-Economy Strategy

For the eighth chapter of *The 33 Strategies of War* entitled "Pick Your Battles Carefully", Greene starts with British Prime Minister Winston Churchill's famous quote where he said, "*You will never achieve your goal in the event that you stop and toss stones at each puppy that barks.*" In an example Greene likes to call "The Winding Effect", he gives a story of Pyrrhus of Epirus who went about as a soldier of fortune to the city of Tarentum, and decided on going to war with Rome. Pyrrhus was drawn into a progression of fights because of his reputation and unfortunately, was guided by deficient insight. He won the fights, yet his armed force was pulverized. The last war, the Pyrrhic War, destroyed him everlastingly and was the beginning of the expression "pyrrhic triumph".

Greene suggests focusing on qualities and weaknesses. He injects the story of Ruler Elizabeth I and how she rose to power in England in the year 1558, around then an optional military power. Against her counselors she paused and did not connect with Philip II of Spain, rather, she searched for more inconspicuous methods for harming him, she enrolled the regal Navy to run privateer attacks on his boats coming back from the New World and utilizing different less customary systems to devastate the Spanish Armada. Ruler Elizabeth I painstakingly picked her fights to preserve assets and gradually pulverize and predominant power.

If you must battle, make sure to battle monetarily, moderating every one of your benefits. Be safe by knowing your qualities and how play them. This is because as a general rule, war comprises of debilitating the opposite side—militarily, monetarily and ethically therefore one must be ready at all times. There are times when one needs to strike in the first place, however attempt to draw your adversary into the principal strike, on your terms. On the off chance that this does not work re-survey your alternatives for a hostile approach. Control your reputation and overlook the irrelevant rest and know the importance of perception management. Try not to give pride a chance to exacerbate your circumstance. Lastly, always remember, as Greene advises, a Pyrrhic triumph will destroy you. Make your fights worth your chance and assets. Your vitality is restricted. Try not to squander it like there is nothing else to do tomorrow.

For this chapter, Greene's "Reversal" states the following key points:

- Manage with what you have. Use your benefits.
- Try not to depend on innovation and gear, depend on your insight.
- Parity your closures to your methods. Try not to get over broadened.
- Utilize trickiness where you don't have the monetary intends to extend.
- Try not to continue just out of pride. Stop before it deteriorates.

- Know your breaking points.

9. Turn the Tables:

The Counterattack Strategy

For the ninth chapter in *The 33 Strategies of War* entitled "Turn the Tables", Greene opens with the story of the 1944 Democratic Presidential race. The Republican Party led by Thomas Dewey, made constant derogatory comments about Franklin Roosevelt, yet he didn't react until the point that they assaulted his puppy, Fala. Roosevelt mortified his rival by protecting his pet companion and uncovering their edgy move for what it was. Roosevelt conveyed a humorous discourse protecting his pooch, mortifying Dewey. Roosevelt was not effortlessly aggravated because he let his adversaries make the primary move, pausing and waiting for his opportunity. Along these lines he could investigate their system and assault his adversaries' shortcomings. In history, protectors are all the more frequently successful than assailants. Frankly stated, people don't care for aggressors, they certainly don't care for spooks. Historically, people show at least a bit of kindness for the casualties of such assaults, notwithstanding when they lay the snare and incite it.

In Greene's example of a "Camouflage Aggression", he tells the story of the pre-engagement in the Battle of Austerlitz (1805) wherein Napoleon played frightened and panicky.

Autocrat Alexander I of Russia, on edge for exact retribution, chose to lead the partners into fight. Napoleon drew the contradicting powers forward to uncover their feeble focus and thrashing them.

The lesson of the chapter is that hazard is inalienable in influencing yourself to look silly and debilitating. Without activity, people will condition individuals to disregard you. You have to make a move once in a while. Remain quiet and transform the circumstance into your support. Moving first demonstrates your adversary your system. Pause; attract them to make the primary move. Investigate their procedure and counterattack in light of the shortcomings they uncover.

For the "Reversals" for this chapter, Greene lists the following:

- History demonstrates that safeguards ordinarily win the war.
- Turn the assailant's outrage against them.
- Expel your feelings.
- Endeavor to draw your adversary into fight by their outrage.
- Resist the urge to panic, disturbing and baffling your adversary.

- Betray your adversary into assaulting.

10. Create a Threatening Presence:

Deterrence Strategies

The tenth chapter of *The 33 Strategies of War* opens with the story of Stonewall Jackson who in 1862 put on an overwhelming show scaring George McClellan amid the American Civil War by indicating the majority of his rivals' blemishes. Greene adds that in the thirteenth century, Robert the Bruce made incredible steps with a ragtag armed force against the British armed forces and King Edward II. His endeavors possible brought him acknowledgment (from King Edward III). The majority of the additions by Robert the Bruce were through strong strikes, quick invasions and mix of hostile and guarded activities. In 1874 Louis XI of France utilized Duke of Milan's diplomat to France, Christopher Bollate, to convey created bits of gossip about France's doubts of the Duke's aims, undermining assault and unreasonable activities. This kept up a serene cooperation. John Boyd was allotted to work in The Pentagon to outline another contender and found the governmental issues troublesome. He utilized a technique of playing moronic, yet vigorously investigating issues purposed by others and plotting strategies to slaughter the activities.

Greene's tenth chapter states that leaders should manufacture

131

the notoriety of being a power of nature, a power to be figured with. Unusualness, frenzy, sudden and strong animosity is terrifying. Plant a seed of uncertainty in your rival's brain and bolster his suspicion. Influence them to trust they can't win and they will withdraw. Influence individuals to figure they will lose, feign if necessary. Individuals need a simple triumph and won't assault on the off chance that they figure they will lose. Be that as it may, be cautious. Your adversary may challenge your blustering, in case you're unwilling to move down your words with activity.

For the "Reversal", the following are the key takeaways:

- Make strong moves and feign shrewdly

- Be a danger, make sudden moves, infer hostility

- Move nonsensically, make unusualness, act insane,

- Feed your rival's neurosis by demonstrating abilities that they fear

- Keep up an awful notoriety, mean, awful and non-debatable

11. Trade Space for Time:
The Nonengagement Strategy

The eleventh chapter of *The 33 Strategies of War* entitled "Trade Space for Time" starts with the remarkable story during the start of the Chinese Civil War where Mao Tse-tung's communists were compelled to withdraw. Chiang Kai-shek's patriot party constrained Mao Tse-tung's communists to withdraw and this activity had the impact of fortifying help for the Communists by joining together and exciting the laborers. In 1949 the communists vanquished the patriots. The communists accepted the open door and assembled bolster by joining the working class, crushing the patriots in 1949 with a chose advantage.

Greene calls this the "Surrender Tactic" wherein one withdraws to advance. Napoleon Bonaparte said "Space we can recoup, time never." Withdraw will pick up the upside of diminishing your rival's powers and stretching their supply and correspondence lines enabling your powers to think. Not battling, when they know you can, will bother your adversary and increment the possibility of them making a nonsensical move. You give your rival a little win keeping in mind the end goal to consume up more room, develop your use and debilitate the adversary before fight. Disappoint them by battling on your terms. This is great Sun Tzu's Art of War material. The adversary gives you pursue you withdraw. The foe withdraws you seek after. It's about the favorable position that decides the final product.

Parts of the "Reversal", the keys to warfare in this chapter are the following:

- Withdraw to cement troops and support.

- Baffle the rival by declining to battle.

- Draw out supply and correspondence lines of rival.

- Make condition for expanded mistake on the rival's side.

PART IV:

OFFENSIVE WARFARE

Greene explains how successful captains in the world's history have practiced the offensive point of view as a strategy. He further explains that this is the type of fighting is an ideal mix of key shrewdness and boldness. The key component comes in the arranging: defining a general objective, creating approaches to achieve it, and thinking the entirety design through in extraordinary detail. This implies thinking regarding a crusade, not singular fights. It additionally implies knowing the qualities and shortcomings of the opposite side, so you can align your strikes to its vulnerabilities. The more nitty-gritty you're arranging, the more certain you will feel as you go into fight, and the simpler it will be to remain on course once the unavoidable issues emerge. In the assault itself, however, you should hit with such soul and boldness that you put your foes on their heels, giving overwhelming force to your hostile.

12. Lose Battles but Win The War:

Grand Strategy

Alexander the Great arranged his campaign far into the future, which recognized him from different pioneers. In the twelfth chapter of The 33 Strategies of War, Greene explains that one of Alexander the Great's intentional objectives was the catching of all more noteworthy Persian Mediterranean ports, successfully leaving the foe without a naval force and removing the ocean segment from future conditions. Alexander the Great built up another procedure of looking far forward, separating him from different pioneers. He initially picked up the ground he required yet did not expand his possessions to a point that they couldn't be administered. He didn't battle fights he couldn't win, for example formulating plans to catch the significant Mediterranean ports; adequately invalidating the Persian naval force.

In addition to the warfare, in the year 1968, amid the Viet Nam war Vo Nguyen Giap executed a nationwide hostile on the Tet occasion. Despite the fact that retreating from their increases, the hostile was planned befuddle the US and South Vietnamese armed forces and to play to the US media.

Greene says that these stories show that it wasn't evident

until the point when it was past the point of no return. Despite the fact that it has turned into an adage; think a few advances. Have a greater campaign and decide the bull's eye, plan to the end and confound your rival abandoning him unfit to peruse your activities, since they don't appear to have an association. At the end of the day, influence them to center around the trees with the goal that they can't see the backwoods. Look past what has all the earmarks of being the danger and discover the source and assault it.

The "Reversals" key points include:

- Make your activities difficult to take after, don't uncover your system.

- Have reason and objective, looking far into what's to come.

- You should be amorphous and hard to peruse, spread false data to lead other's off track.

13.   Know Your Enemy:

The Intelligence Strategy

In the vicinity of 1806 and 1813 Prince Metternich met with Napoleon with expectations of understanding him and discovering purposes of shortcoming that he could misuse. Ruler Metternich met Napoleon Bonaparte trusting he could locate his frail spots. A couple of years after the fact he had organized Napoleon's marriage to Marie Louise, who wasn't the most charming spouse. In the end he helped with coordinating Napoleon's marriage to Marie Louise. Metternich utilized this and other information to the upside of Austria enabling them to manufacture an armed force and join a more noteworthy partnership in Europe in the long run prompting the thrashing of Napoleon at Waterloo. Napoleon's annihilation at Waterloo had additionally been crafted by Metternich's spying without trying to hide.

In this thirteenth chapter, Greene adds that in 1838, the British attack of Afghanistan was to reestablish western agreeable Shuja Shah Durrani, ousting the present pioneer Dost Mohammad Khan. Be that as it may, Auckland did not comprehend the Afghan individuals or their way of life, committing various errors. The outcome was his demise and the arrival of Dost Mohammad to control.

Ace non-verbal correspondence, shroud your perceptions and devise the best strategies in view of your bits of knowledge. Know thyself and know thy equal. One of the best aptitudes in war, as in temptation as in business is the capacity to peruse individuals. Know your adversary's moves and don't give your intentions a chance to be known.

"Reversals" for this chapter include:

- Accumulate information of your rival.

- Figure out how to peruse individuals, learn them.

- Shroud your perceptions.

- Take a stab at nature of data, not amount.

- Know about inner government agents and incapacitate them.

- Submerge yourself in their psyche.

- Moderate whimsical begin that is non-prescient, speed is basic.

139

14. Overwhelm Resistance with Speed and Suddenness: The Blitzkrieg Strategy

In 1218, the first Great Khan of the Mongol empire, Genghis Khan conquered his adversary, the person who should not be named, with The Blitzkrieg Strategy. Khan portioned his powers for portability, lost little fights intentionally, at that point moved to genuine and quick assaults, which the adversary had not expected.

Greene suggests that a person should moderate speedy brisk by making moderate moves to set the pace to which your adversary modifies, at that point abuse the Überraschungs moment to win the war rapidly. Moderate deliberate begin with an all-around arranged assault, move quick and beyond any doubt.

The fourteenth chapter does not a have solid "Reversal", rather, Greene states that a person or leader should have full control, despite the fact that he might not have any desire to indicate it.

15. Control the Dynamic:

Forcing Strategies

In 1942 amid the second World War, Erwin Rommel battled the British on the North African deserts, utilizing littler units, keeping them progressing and out of the rival's span. With a specific end goal to lessen the hole amongst occasions and notices he'd frequently join the bleeding edge.

Greene also adds several stories more in the book's fifteenth chapter, and seconds with Mae West who while taking a shot at the Paramount Pictures film Night After Night, in 1932, she gradually rolled out moves to improvement the dynamic of energy into her court. In the long run she assumed control critical bits of the movies composing.

In addition, amid the American Civil War, General Sherman went head to head with General Johnston in fights over Richmond, Virginia. He played to Johnston's distrustfulness and his general cautious nature. He proceeded with the strategies against General Hood in Atlanta, Georgia and took the city in an unexpected move.

Similarly, the slave Frederick Douglass, initially possessed by Thomas Auld, was sent to be "broken" by Edward Covey. After numerous fights, Douglass turned out to be straightforwardly resistant to Covey, dreading passing and having nothing to lose Covey battled Covey and accomplished triumph basically by making a circumstance where Covey would lose his notoriety for being a slave breaker.

Therapist Milton H. Erickson utilized hypnotherapy among different methods, to help his patients. Every so often his patients would not collaborate with his treatment. He would pick up control through different means including entrancing, double dealing and inversion.

Greene states that as a leader, you're in charge. Be confident and explore your rival by compelling him to move, specifically into your territory of barrier. The main drawback to control may be not conceding that you have it. Influence the primary move, to battle on your domain where you are agreeable, search for your adversary's shortcoming and draw them into it, beguile your rival to influence them to think they are in charge.

16. Hit Them Where It Hurts:

The Center-of-Gravity Strategy

The sixteenth chapter of *The 33 Strategies of War* is timely short, sweet and direct to the point. Greene, like all chapters, starts with a remarkable story. In 209 BC Publius Scipio vanquished Nova Carthago, which was the Carthaginian capital in Spain. Scipio wrecked Hannibal's armed forces' fundamental supply lines. Inside 5 years Scipio caught Carthage and finished Hannibal's adventure. Scipio proceeded to Carthage in 204 BC, catching it in 203 BC reviewing Hannibal from Italy and evacuating his danger.

The chapters' strategy is to take a hold of and unbalance the rest of the structure, cutting supply lines, conviction frameworks and leadership hierarchies. Assault the essential issue, be it the war room, supply lines, conviction framework. Catch and obliterate it. Locate the inside purpose of your rival and assault it—be it correspondence, media, supply lines. Isolating your group can produce a deft and versatile power.

17.   Defeat Them In Detail:

The Divide-And-Conquer Strategy

Separation et Impera - the Divide and Conquer Strategy which most people have heard of. The most common phrase heard in computer games and sometimes cliché, Greene uses this strategy to theorize his skill of being keen to details. He starts with the story of the Persians in the year 490 BC. The Persians arrived on the fields of Marathon 24 miles close Athens, part their armed force during the evening, intending to assault Athens via ocean. The Greeks assaulted the rest of the Persians, at that point ran all they route back to Athens to shield the city.

In what Greene calls "Assaulting the Joints", the authors adds the story of Samuel Adams. Paving the way to the American Revolution, Adams was persistently battling for the free portrayal for the settlements. Generally he battled, until the point that the institution of the Stamp Act by the British. In 1765 Adams could rally the homesteaders around the purpose of "No imposing taxes without any political benefit". At that point with the Tea Act, in 1773, Adams revived individuals to revolt, dumping tea into the Boston Harbor.

Take a gander at the parts and decide how to control the

individual parts, make disagreement and use it. This is the starting point of "running a marathon." Gap vast units and they're less demanding targets. At the point when your foes are on edge, they will endeavor to join together and confront you with their full power. You don't permit them such quality.

18. Expose and Attack Your Opponents
Soft Flank: The Turning Strategy

In 1796 Napoleon Bonaparte goaded Baron Joseph Alvinczy into charging forward, subsequently uncovering his armed forces flank. This was the open door Napoleon had sought after, encompassing and overcoming his rival again.

Julius Caesar idealized the craft of backhanded battling. In spite of the fact that there were commonly when he enrolled the immediate technique, there are numerous situations where he battled in a roundabout way. Outstandingly were the power battles with Pompey. Quite a bit of his work was finished by demonstrating Pompey's men his generosity and fair treatment of his troops. This attempted to get a significant number of his rival's troops to surrender.

Greene suggests drawing for a frontal assault; getting your adversary to broaden his positions and in the diversion have your powers assaults his uncovered flank or back. Perplex your opponent, influence him to bring down his defenses through indirection, at that point convey an effective hit to his uncovered and helpless side. Utilize appeal and blandishment to draw you rival to lower defenses. Demonstrate your adversary's awful attributes.

146

19. Envelop the Enemy:

The Annihilation Strategy

In 1778 the Zulu warriors battled the British in Natal forcing them with shock assaults all of a sudden by knowing their home domain by heart. In the Battle of Isandlwana the Zulu utilized their insight into the land to encompass shock and defeat the British.

On the other hand, John D. Rockefeller utilized this strategy consistently to "encompass" potential rivalry by purchasing area and framework they expected to contend with him.

Utilize what you have in plenitude. Keep up steady weight on your adversary to overcome their determination. Encasing the rival completes a number on his psychological prosperity. Feeling caught they will withdraw, on the off chance that they can. Make the sentiment being encompassed by making assaults from no place. There is no preferred standpoint of an immediate assault. Moving, however, can give you an excessive number of alternatives and can deaden your progress.

20. Maneuver Them into Weakness:

The Ripening-For-The-Sickle Strategy

The twentieth chapter of *The 33 Strategies of War* entitled "Maneuver Them into Weakness" starts with the remarkable story of Bokuden; an ace samurai who was honing the craft of "winning without hands" was tested by a youthful swordsman. Bokuden chose they ought to have the duel on an island. When the swordsman left the watercraft, the grandmaster pushed it far from the shore, leaving the youthful warrior stranded.

Greene adds that in 1800, Napoleon needed to crush the Austrian armed forces in Italy. He made his arrangements and about everything turned out badly. However, Napoleon had sufficiently made exchange arrangements and he continued moving to the new circumstances close by and he vanquished them at Marengo where is unique designs had anticipated he would.

In the 1936 US Presidential crusade the Republican Party designated Alf Landon to keep running against occupant Franklin D. Roosevelt (D). Landon endeavored to overcome Roosevelt by supporting the New Deal however condemning the maker (FDR). Roosevelt held up until the point that Landon did not have enough time to move from this position and assaulted.

148

In World War I the British attempted to catch Aqaba from the Turks. T. E. Lawrence, conversant in Arabic and acquainted with the clans of the Syrian Desert, utilized a little armed force to move rapidly through the desert and estrange the Turks. His quick moving denied the Turks an objective and he could cut their supply lines bringing about the surrender of Aqaba.

In 1937 Harry Cohn of Columbia Pictures procured Leo McCarey to coordinate The Awful Truth The content was poor and McCarey needed to make sense of how to enhance the content. He routinely rolled out improvements at last and would hold up to shoot until the point that he felt it was correct. This ploy gave the motion picture suddenness and drove it to progress.

Make adaptable plans with numerous alternatives. Continue ascertained moves in your position. This will empower you to control the circumstance and confuse and deplete your rival. Outflank the rival, dodging an advantage-less direct assault, through ascertained moves, which concede you more prominent control over the current circumstance. Make arrangements that hold your rival under tight restraints and dependably on another protective.

21. Negotiate While Advancing:

The Diplomatic-War Strategy

In 359 BC Alexander the Great's dad Philip II of Macedonia came to reign, Athens declining to remember him. He talked about peace and thriving as he kept on growing his domain joining other Greek city-states to lead an assault on the Persians.

In the beginning of the Greek War of Independence, year 1821, the Russia's Greek conceived remote pastor Capo d'Istria felt it basic that Russia bolsters Greece. This would give Russia access to warm water ports in the Mediterranean. Careful about the craving of Austria's Prince Metternich to keep Russia from these ports, he forewarned his emissary to not give Metternich a chance to arrange. This fizzled and Metternich played to the shortcomings of Czar Alexander I and he impeded endeavors of Russia helping Greece.

22. When arranging a settlement you ought not to let up on the strain to progress. This furnishes you more to consult with and does not give your adversary time to regroup. Arrange, willing to go to a win-win course of action, yet continue moving concentrating on your association's advance. You maintain a strategic distance from

quick clash, while encouraging your interests.

Your requests are strong, yet perpetually

sensible, as your shadow develops.

How to End Things: The Exit Strategy

The twenty second chapter of *The 33 Strategies of War* opens with the story of Lyndon Johnson. In 1937, Johnson won the race for a Texas Congressional seat with the assistance of his companions in the gathering, overcoming the more established and experienced legislators. Not squandering a moment he unassumingly took to them, said thanks to them and communicated his desires for future joint effort, effectively.

The Soviet Union's attack of Afghanistan, and the subsequent war, caused a hopeless scenario for the Soviet Union principally because of the absence of comprehension of the Afghan individuals.

Know when you are beat and cut your losses. Know how to win with energy and convey a positive conclusion to the experience; diminishing your adversaries later on. Greene explains that people should try not to confide in individuals' words. Visionaries never entire, their end is constantly poor. He instills that they will break their guarantees and discovers moral legitimizations for their flippant practices. Individuals will overlook broken guarantees when a person offers solid and is willing to offer something this other person needs. Finish up understanding the end is more imperative than the accomplishment of the battle. The author also says that for a person to continue winning the war, they will need to show signs of improvement arrangements that they can utilize as negotiating concessions.

PART V:

UNCONVENTIONAL (DIRTY) WARFARE

In the fifth and last part of The 33 Strategies of War, Greene gives a small introduction on what to expect in the last chapters. He explains that a general battling a war should continually scan for favorable position over the rival. Additionally, Greene suggests that the best preferred standpoint originates from the component of shock, from hitting adversaries with procedures that are novel, outside their encounter, totally capricious. It is in the idea of war, be that as it may, that after some time any technique with any conceivable application will be attempted and tried, so the scan for the new and eccentric has an intrinsic propensity to wind up increasingly outrageous. In the meantime, Greene states that moral and moral codes that represented fighting for a considerable length of time have continuously extricated. These two impacts dovetail into what we today call "grimy war," where anything goes, down to the murdering of thousands of unwarned regular folks.

23. Weave a Seamless Blend of Fact and Fiction: Misperception Strategies

How things end is the only thing that is in any way important. What's more, the completion is your last judge. Greene talks about the sand traps of extended wars with not a single end to be seen, similar to the Russians in Afghanistan or the Americans in Vietnam for the book's twenty-third chapter. Amid readiness for the attack at Normandy in World War II, the partners built up a critical number of beguiling plans. These incorporated a phony armed force in England (FUSAG) and a carbon copy of General Montgomery in the Mediterranean theater. An abundance of falsehood, deadened Hitler's basic leadership abilities when the real intrusion began, moderated his response.

Greene suggests cutting your misfortunes and moving out when you see that annihilation is unavoidable, you can attempt to go down in style. Planting the seeds of future triumph amid annihilation is technique of the most elevated request. Consider it to be a transitory annihilation, welcome it as an approach to make yourself more grounded, and as an approach to show your character and your quality to remain cheery even in misfortune. The best component of amazement is utilizing new procedures that no one anticipates. As individuals push for curiosity however, says Greene, there's a race to the extremes, prompting dirtier wars. Deception is an old craftsmanship and priceless while diverting individuals from your track. Deception and baits can devour your adversary. Be that as it may, you should go messy yourself. You can't chance misfortune out of a feeling of ethical quality.

"Reversals" for this chapter include:

- Make a solid front look feeble.

- Make a frail front look solid and assault from another course.

- Bolster your rival with deception.

- Keep up an example with the purpose of transforming it for shock.

- Utilize creative and finish disguise.

- Make the genuine look false and the false look genuine to make finish vagueness.

- There is no preferred standpoint to assaulting by the normal means and strategies

24. Take the Line of Least Expectation:

The Ordinary-Extraordinary Strategy

Duplicity isn't tied in with making enormous shows of expand diversions. A great many people know you'll endeavor to swindle them and won't get bulldozed by it. The best misdirection blends reality with fiction. Greene included chronicled examples for this chapter including:

For the New York Society of Independent Artists' first show, Marcel Duchamp picked a radical new arrangement—anybody could display a masterpiece. Duchamp under the nom de plume. Mutt" presented a urinal laying on its back called the Fountain. There was shock in the association, however opened another view and tested the meaning of craftsmanship.

In 219 BC Rome choose to attack with Hannibal. They confronted him at the Trebia waterway. Hannibal showed sporadic conduct drew the Roman armed force over the stream and after that stunned them with his utilization of elephants. The Romans made numerous different endeavors to draw Hannibal into a battle however Hannibal did the opposite they expected giving him an incredible preferred standpoint.

In 1862 Ulysses S. Concede, American Civil War General drove a fight to catch Vicksburg, Mississippi. He moved troops over the Mississippi River and sent them toward Jackson to slice the supply lines to Vicksburg. This move was not expected since it would imply that Grant's powers would not have their correspondence lines open. It astounded Confederate General John C. Pemberton; who was not able foresee the effect of the move.

Cassius Clay tested then Heavyweight champion Sonny Liston to the enclosing 1962. title. Earth's irregular conduct and battling method and his free thinker conduct gave him an extraordinary preferred standpoint in the battle since his adversary did not realize what's in store.

The Ojibwa clan had a tip top band of warriors called the Wendigokan. This band would act insane amid fights, hollering the correct inverse of their purpose. This caused perplexity in their rivals and panicked them not to take part in fight.

Do the unforeseen. On the off chance that constantly quiet be radical, if constantly radical accomplish something standard. Spread your double dealings to individuals who have confidence in the lie themselves, and they'll work to persuade others, normally, of your trickiness. Playing the high

158

ground can influence you to look honest and deigning. This can distance and sicken your supporters. At last, make up substances that match your foe's craving and they'll swindle themselves into trusting it.

"Reversals" and Key Takeaways for this chapter are the following:

- Utilize strategies that your rival does not know.

- Blend conventional strategies with the bizarre.

- Act insane however computed.

- Keep on thinking of new things.

25. Occupy the Moral High Ground:

`The Righteous Strategy

Greene says that the best broad have a touch of vital frenzy. As we age however we have a tendency to fit in with old propensities to an ever increasing extent, and that is the means by which Napoleon declined and came to depend more on estimate than on splendid technique. The author suggests it is best to take the moral offensive like Pope Leo X. When the mentioned Pope needed to finish development of St. Dwindle's Basilica, he began the act of offering liberalities to raise the assets for the congregation. German scholar and Priest named Martin Luther tested the practices in the 95 Theses saying that no one but God could excuse one's wrongdoings. He contended his stand construct exclusively in light of the Bible deliberately disproving every one of the Pope's answers. This exertion by Martin Luther was the beginning of the Lutheran and Protestant customs.

You can't utilize regular means with a guerrilla you should deny them targets. On the off chance that you do assault, assault solid and fast at any main issue they have. Justify your motivation as the right and good way. Demonstrate your adversary's self-serving side. Show yourself as the underdog. Keep an edge of eccentric rather and bring an end to the propensities.

Key Takeaways from the twenty-fifth chapter include:

- Uncover the pietism of your adversary.

- Legitimize your activities in view of ethical quality.

- Speak to yourself as "great", your rival as "terrible".

- A corrupt demonstration will destroy your notoriety.

- Make your rival begin the real "battle".

- Wars of self-intrigue are short and characterized.

26. Deny Them Targets:

The Strategy of the Void

Greene sets the "Lure of the Void" with the encounter of Napoleon's 1812 attack of Russia met with a withdrawing Russian armed force setting up little opposition and purchasing time. Cossacks killed him, withdrawing Russian troops abandoned wore out towns and fields and no nourishment. The underlying French power of 450,000 troops was decreased to 100,000 when they achieved Moscow.

Influence your motivation to appear to be ethically defended and paint your foe as shrewd. Provoke an adversary you can depict as ethically degenerate. Remove any objectives you have for your adversaries. Try not to make a front or make your front so wide that assaulting it assaults their base. No objectives will baffle your rivals expanding the shot they will commit an error. Try not to rustle up your ethical prevalence yet demonstrate it: balance your own existence with theirs. Be careful about individuals that provide to your with some much needed help. Other will utilize this against you; guarantee that they don't utilize you contrarily.

27.   Seem to Work for the Interests of Others While Furthering Your Own:

The Alliance Strategy

In 1467 Charles I, Duke of Burgundy extended his domain by framing an organization together with Edward IV of England to assault Louis XI of France. In any case, King Louis XI got some answers concerning the intrusion and framed collusion with Edward IV expelling the risk from the Duke.

Murray Bowen, on the other hand is a therapist, who utilized his clinical information to determine an individual family circumstance. He composed a progression of letters to relatives keeping in mind the end goal to demonstrate worry for the individual, however uncovering an arrangement on gossipy relations that were in the family. In this procedure he really made a level of self-governance for himself which enabled him to control the circumstance and encourage his kin in making a sound family relationship.

Be that as it may, it's not valid: the more you have, the more probable it is you'll be dragged into other individuals' wars. Collusions must be founded on shared interests. Consider them to be venturing stones towards getting what you require.

163

The vast majority work with sentiments and feelings and make unions in view of loving and kinships. Not genuine: the best cooperation are the ones giving something you can't get individually. Give your adversaries a chance to pursue you into vacancy. Abstain from battling, give them no objective. At long last, never turn out to be excessively subject to cooperation: they will drop you when it best serves them. Collusions Strategies: Appear like you need to help and let them take every necessary step; at that point receive the rewards.

28. Give Your Rival Enough Hope To Hang Themselves:

The One-Upmanship Strategy

Now and then adversaries are your associates, your teammates. Greene gives authentic examples with several interesting stories that are examples of offbeat fighting getting it done as they all attempt to keep appearance of working for more prominent benefit.

John McClernand volunteered as a Brigadier General in the American Civil War. He needed distinction and rising to the administration. He took a stab at utilizing his impact with President Abraham Lincoln to attempt to assume control over the attack of Vicksburg, Mississippi. General Grant, whose division Vicksburg fell under, found out about the plans and occupied troops make a beeline for McClernand for his own utilization. This and different activities maddened McClernand, whom made various moves that estranged him from his partners.

Joan Crawford had a nonstop contention with Norma Shearer and Bette Davis. She imagined two techniques for stealing their thunder. With Shearer she attempted to disturb her on set and motivated her to uncover her awful manner. While with Davis, she stole the spotlight while tolerating

Anne Bancroft's Oscar for The Miracle Worker.

Tsukahara Bokuden, prestigious samurai, was tested by an able to use both hands youthful samurai. Bokuden acknowledged the test, however concentrated on the "unjustifiable" utilization of his left arm. In the battle, Bokuden assaulted his right. Afterward, in 1605, the swordsman Genzaemon was tested by Miyamoto Musashi. Musashi appeared late and in non-standard clothing, this infuriated Genzaemon situating him to make numerous errant moves.

Sway Dole of Kansas tested George H. W. Hedge for the 1988 Republican's designation for President. Lee Atwater, Bush's strategist, knowing about Dole's temper, spread gossipy tidbits about his wife's, Elizabeth Dole, capabilities as Secretary of Transportation. Doles outrage came through in the media seriously harming him.

Académie Française was established in 1635 to keep up the virtue of the French dialect. In 1694 King Louis IV delegated the Bishop of Noyons to the insight. Albeit qualified, he was haughty and hostile. On introduction day the abbé de Caumartin gave an inconspicuously ridiculing discourse that was viewed accordingly by everything except the Bishop. His possible mortification prompted the Bishop leaving the

Académie.

Give your adversaries the space to commit errors, give them assignments they can't finish and harm their notoriety. Shroud your association and keep up your blameless. Try not to assault them head on: it will just influence you to look terrible. Get under their skin unobtrusively. Inflexible composes who can't stand breaking moral codes are the simplest to one-up. Utilize others to work the uneasiness and make it greater. Get the adversary to over-respond and advance back and let them wrap up. They will blow up and assault you too clearly, influencing them to look noxious. It works best with individuals who need to execute as they won't have the capacity to be taking care of business. Ingrain questions and weaknesses in rivals, inspiring them to think excessively and act protective. Influence them to hang themselves through their own reckless inclinations, abandoning you faultless and clear. Search for the inner opponent, locate their powerless spot and needle it to make them on edge. When they are close to the finish of their annihilation offer assistance, not to rub in the thrashing, but rather help demonstrate your honesty.

29. Take Small Bites:

The Fait Accompli Strategy

A great many people stick to existing conditions and are disinclined of beginning wars once again trifling issues. Greene imposes that is the reason you will take little chomps, nibble by chomp. Each time it will be too little to begin a war and once you take enough nibbles they won't have the capacity to take up arms against you.

The author narrates the story of wherein upon the fall of France to the Germans in World War II, Charles de Gaulle got authorization from Winston Churchill to communicate to the Fighting French over the BBC. The communication was met with incredible open help. He kept on growing this little toehold by driving powers in Central Africa, assembling the French Resistance with Jean Moulin. At the point when FDR's plotted to supplant him with Henri Giraud, de Gaulle battled sharply with Giraud and could fill his staff with de Gaulle followers.

Greene suggests to make propels by little pieces, frequently going unnoticed by your adversaries. When they see your development, it might be past the point of no return.

168

30. Penetrate Their Minds:

Communication Strategies

The objective of correspondence is to promote your enthusiasm, to enter the adversaries' psyches. Influence individuals to achieve your decisions and let them trust it was their own thoughts. Greene adds that in shooting *The 39 Steps* in 1935, Alfred Hitchcock bound the leads Madeleine Carroll and Robert Donat and after that bluffed losing the key and left them cuffed.

In fact, Adolf Hitler doled out Wilhelm Canaris to set up the Abwehr in late 1933. Hitler was awed and believed him for counsel amid his residency he educated against the attack concerning the United Kingdom, instructed against aligning with Francisco Franco regarding Spain to utilize the island of Gibraltar to debilitate the British and guaranteed Hitler that Italy's Pietro Badoglio was not going to surrender in 1943..

In addition is the story of André Breton, maker of the Surrealist Manifesto, needed to inhale more life into the surrealistic development. He felt Salvador Dalí could give that lift. It did. Be that as it may, Dali's partiality to Hitler and Lenin heated the gathering to the point of boiling. Dali left for New York where he made an effective profession and ended up synonymous with surrealism.

Exceptionally fascinating investigation of The Prince here by Robert Greene and how additionally composing must be engaged to spreading your plans to be powerful. Invade your adversary's camp. Once there, you don't have to assault or demonstrate your aims. Gradually assume control from inside. Fight with words that will possess your adversary, influence them to think and endeavor to decipher your significance. Utilize activities other than words, when required, to establish a long term connection.

31. Destroy From Within:

The Inner-Front Strategy

Rather than battling your adversaries, Greene suggests to go along with them. Penetrate their positions, ascend to the best. At that point gradually get what you need or stage an overthrow.

The case presented in the thirty-first chapter of *The 33 Strategies of War* was that of Canaris, a high positioning officer in Hitler's covert operative systems. Fundamentally this person was one of the greatest impacts in the Nazi's misfortune and no history books have ever specified him.

Greene also adds the story of how Mahatma Gandhi organized a 200 mile walk off to the sea. The Governor-General of India, Lord Edward Irwin, was calmed at the appearing to be unimportant activity Gandhi proposed. Ruler Edward Irwin did nothing to stop the walk. Yet, the walk pulled in thousands. Irwin had restricted his alternatives since he had not acted ahead of schedule to stop the walk and now it would be a major issue. Gandhi had picked his challenge carefully—amiable to the British and strong to the Indians.

Use non-hostility to battle your rival. Their forceful demonstrations will profit you and accumulate bolster from others. Since there is the introduction of both "great" and "awful" qualities, individuals ordinarily observe just the positive approach.

32. Dominate While Seeming To Submit:

The Passive-Aggression Strategy

In the thirty-second chapter of *The 33 Strategies of War*, Greene suggests to appear to submit and oblige. Mask your animosity so you can deny it even exists. Individuals are not very much prepared to see both animosity and accommodation in the meantime and will normally simply oblige one. In a clever and swift manner, Greene uses the tale of Roosevelt where former president imagined he would not like to keep running for a third time, so no one could blame him for being power hungry. At the point when individuals requested him, he showed up nearly as though he needed to oblige.

In a world that loathes full animosity; inactive hostility is on the ascent. It's likewise hard to battle individuals who battle without brutality. On the off chance that your adversary assaults, they will look awful and legitimize additionally revolts. In the event that they let you go, you can develop your clout. Above all else, dispense with any sentiment blame you may have when they demonstrate the aloof side. At whatever point you can, separate. When you can't never assault specifically yet utilize their strategies back.

33. Sow Uncertainty and Panic through Acts of Terror: The Chain-Reaction Strategy

For the last chapter of *The 33 Strategies of War*, Greene tells his peruser to dread systems and go for raising destruction, making foes frightful and inciting frantic overcompensations - or surrenders without battling.

Greene tells the story of Nizam al-Mulk who was at first felt to be a backlash for the endeavors to smother the development of the organization Nizari Ismaili. The Nizari, a gathering shrouded in mystery, had built up another strategy for revolt where Assassins would rise up out of an apparently quiet group and slaughter their objective with a knife. They work well for to littler gatherings that can't battle transparently in light of size dissimilarity. Another example Greene notes is that of Mongols and the spreading stories of their repulsions so adversaries would surrender without a battle.

The objective is confusion and making the absence of trust in commonplace environment. What was once protected is currently questionable. Counterstrategies incorporate resisting the urge to panic and normal and estranging the fear bunches

174

from the majority to deny any political base. They will likely spread dread with little demonstrations of brutality that resound through stories and media and charge outsized consideration contrasted with their genuine impact. Preventing the fear from spreading is additionally critical and overwhelming military commitment from the more grounded side is frequently an error.

Conclusion

While it is completely hard to summarize and conclude Robert Greene's *The 33 Strategies of War* in one single area of this book, it is without a doubt he is a master in what he writes about. This critically acclaimed novel will arm a man with the understanding that pushes him to participate in the dens of corporate battles and war. Thusly, readers suggestively consolidate this novel with those of Machiavelli's "*The Prince*", and one has both the mental devices and philosophical comprehension to build up a mind blowing competency in tricky.

What sets this novel apart from most is the book's explicit storyline wherein Greene provides a story to tell for each theory. He carefully and cleverly injects a historical piece that would give an relatable analogy for each strategy he sets and remarkably draws the mind to believe each word he puts in. Being the world class author he is known very well for, Greene sets another record for his published books, making him the master of seduction, strategy and management.

Considered to be a bible for every corporate leader, manager or executive, The 33 Strategies of War is a complete guide on how to be effective in order to drive the best results and benefit from them. Greene creates this guideline so that his peruser can have their cake and well, eat them too.

Beside its important early parts on self-coordinated fighting, the book is filled to the overflow with sections on association, collecting helpful partners, sowing disarray into the positions of your foes, keeping your camaraderie's high, et cetera. The sections on singular techniques are regularly loaded with point by point records. The section on resolve is especially keen for trying expert persuaders. One understanding on persuading your subordinates, originating from Hannibal, fills in as a decent review of what's in store. Each area contains its own procedures, laid out from demonstrated outcomes on renowned combat zones, as well as in ordinary fights. How Alfred Hitchcock defeated interfering makers to hold a heavenly control of his movies is a story told and additionally well as how the Russians crushed Napoleon's armed force by declining to connect with it every step of the way.

Yet again, Greene unleashes his writing prowess in this book and shows the entire universe that one may go to war, equipped with the right set of strategies, or 33 rather; anyone can survive the corporate jungle.

Final Thoughts

Hey! Did you enjoy this book? We sincerely hope you thoroughly enjoyed this short read and have gotten immensely valuable insights that will help you in any areas of your life.

Would it be too greedy if we ask for a review from you?

It takes 1 minute to leave 1 review to possibly influence 1 more person's decision to read just 1 book which may change their 1 life. Your 1 minute matters and we value it and thank you so much for giving us your 1 minute. If it sucks, just say it sucks. Period.

FREE BONUS

P.S. Is it okay if we overdeliver?

Here at Abbey Beathan Publishing, we believe in overdelivering way beyond our reader's expectations. Is it okay if we overdeliver?

Here's the deal, we're going to give you an extremely valuable cheatsheet of "Accelerated Learning". We've partnered up with Ikigai Publishing to present to you the exclusive bonus of "Accelerated Learning Cheatsheet"

What's the catch? We need to trust you... You see, we want to overdeliver and in order for us to do that, we've to trust our reader to keep this bonus a secret to themselves. Why? Because we don't want people to be getting our exclusive accelerated learning cheatsheet without even buying our books itself. Unethical, right?

Ok. Are you ready?

Simply Visit this link: http://bit.ly/acceleratedcheatsheet

We hope you'll enjoy our free bonuses as much as we've enjoyed preparing it for you!

Free Bonus #2: Free Book Preview of Summary: Dreams from my Father

The Book at a Glance

Chapter 1 is all about Barack Obama's origins. He was born to a white mother and a black African father. His grandparents were witness to racial discrimination in the past, and their being liberal-minded and how they respected "colored" people led to his parents union. Although Barack's father left them when he was only 2 years old, his mother and grandparents never spoke ill of him. They still remembered and shared their memories of him as a dignified, intelligent, and graceful gentleman.

Chapter 2 talks about how Barack immigrated to Indonesia when his mother married an Indonesian. In the new country, he turned to his stepfather Lolo for guidance and advice. He learned how to survive, and learned life-long values such as honesty, fairness, and being straightforward. He was also exposed to the cruel world of poverty and violence.

Chapter 3 brings him back to America, where he was required to go to school. His mother stayed in Indonesia with Lolo and his new sister, Maya. She would later join him in America. He would also meet his father for the first time since he left. He would live with him for a month and get to know the father that he never knew.

Chapter 4 shares how Barack went through high school and his experiences living with his grandparents. In fact, he had an eye-opening experience when his grandmother was harassed by a black man on the way to work. As a result, he turned to books trying to search for answers to his identity and on the roots of racism.

In chapter 5, Barack, having found his voice, became active in school rallies. During this time, his mother talked him into building a future by starting college. He would turn to one of his gramps' friends, Frank the poet, and would be warned to keep his eyes open. It was a difficult time, and he further experienced an identity crisis.

In chapter 6, Barack takes the opportunity of a transfer program to Columbia University and transfers to Manhattan. He stays with a Pakistani friend who was an illegal immigrant and became serious about his studies. During the summer, when his mother visited him with Maya, his sister, he would learn of the true story behind his parents' separation and would serve as a realization. He would carry his father's memories even after his death and find a new identity for himself in light of his father.

Chapter 7 talks about how Barack was inspired to become an organizer. He was promoted as a financial writer but later resigned his post. At first, his dreams of becoming an organizer slipped away, if not for his half-sister's phone call that gave him a push. He got hired by a Jewish organizer, Marty Kaufman, and set off to Chicago.

Chapter 8 shows Barack's first few days as an organizer in Chicago.

He attended the CCRC rally, which composed of people who were laid off from work. The first few days were full of challenges as there was trouble talking to people and coming up with an issue that everyone believed was worth fighting for.

In chapter 10, Barack was almost ready to give up. However, his and his co-organizers realizations motivated him to do better and make a difference. In the end, he was successful in organizing a meeting with the Mayor's Office Employment and Training (MET), and the result was a promise to have a MET intake center within the vicinity in six months' time.

Chapter 10 speaks of winter, which was a time of realization for Barack. From the stories he heard from the organization leaders, he realized that they were fighting for a cause due to their past – just like him. This led him to open up and relate better to others.

Barack finally meets his half-sister from Kenya, named Auma, in chapter 11. During her visit, she told him things about their father, which made him get to know him from another's point of view. It was in this reunion with her sister that he finally felt free from the memories of his father.

Chapter 12 talks about the success Barack was finally making as an organizer. He eventually separated ways with this boss, Marty. They were able to launch the new MET intake center in Roseland, and also get some young parents involved in fighting for health causes.

In chapter 13, Barack employed a recruit named Johnnie, whom he got along well. He also visited his half-brother in Washington, D.C., and learned more from him. However, Roy's attitude towards their father was more of bitterness.

Chapter 14 talks about how Barack decided to pursue law at Harvard and selected Johnnie to replace him as lead organizer. Their current project was to target the public schools with the help of religious congregations. Barack attended his first ever service and was moved to tears with the realization of hope.

Chapter 15 brings Barack to Kenya, where he meets British men on the plane who were to make up for the "lack of trained professionals" in Kenya. He managed to have his luggage accidentally sent to Johannesburg, and was helped by a lovely stewardess who knew his father. He felt a sense of belonging in Kenya, but the locals still saw him as American.

In chapter 16, Barack meets his other relatives and learns of the rift among his two aunts, Zeituni and Sarah, due to his father's inheritance. He also meets with his half-brother, seventeen-year-old Bernard. Later on, he would meet his father's other wife, Ruth, and his stepbrother Mark, who also studies in America.

Chapter 17 is a family reunion, when Roy comes home to Kenya earlier than expected. Barack and Auma had just come back from a safari, and he was enjoying the last few days of his vacation.

Chapter 18 introduces more of Barack's extended family. He met his grandmother, two uncles, and his grandfather's brother. He also noticed that people would always ask him for something when he arrived. His relatives highly regarded him due to his father's stories about him.

In chapter 19, Barack learns more about his grandfather's discipline and how he prospered due to hard work, about his father's diligence to study abroad, and about the events that happened to his father. He finally understood and felt complete.

The epilogue fast-forwards to the future. Barack pursued law and gave back to the community by helping out community organizers and churches. He met his future wife, Michelle, who was immediately loved by his family. They got married despite some deaths in both their families.

Part 1: Origins

Chapter 1

Barack Obama was named after his father, who was an African
Kenyan and a member of the Luo tribe. His father was a smart man
who won a scholarship in Nairobi and was among the chosen few
who attended university in the United States. He was the first
African student at the University of Hawaii, where he graduated at
the top of his class, and became president of the International
Students Association. He also met his future wife in Hawaii.
However, he was asked to go back to Africa for his duties. His son,
Barack or Barry, was only two years old at that time. Mother and
son remained in the United States.

Barack Junior's mother and grandparents talked fondly of his father.
His grandparents told him of a story wherein a white man at the bar
was being racist and tried to humiliate his father. His father lectured
the man. As a result, the man tried to buy his forgiveness. When
Barack was 21, his aunt Jane, who had been a stranger until then,
called from Nairobi. She announced that his father had died in a car
crash.

One of the things that Barack wondered about was why his
mother's parents permitted her to marry his father. Barack's mother
was white, and his father was African and black. Eventually, he
learned that his grandparents were raised in decent and respectable

families, so discrimination was not known. His grandparents also told stories about their past, which were filled with romance, drama, and action. In fact, the stories were always interesting. He also learned that his grandparents eloped just before the Pearl Harbor bombing and that his grandfather enlisted in the army.

His grandfather was also the adventurous type who loved to venture on new starts. He was also poetic and a freethinker. This liberal-mindedness paved the way for his father's invitation to dinner. When Barack's mother invited his father for dinner, his grandfather was struck by his resemblance to his favorite singer, Nat King Cole. When dinner ended, his grandparents commented how dignified, intelligent, and graceful he was – and he also loved his British accent.

When the family moved to Texas, they had their experiences with racial discrimination. These incidents explained why his grandparents allowed his white mother to marry a black man. First was when his grandmother, called Toot or Tutu, spoke with a World War II veteran who was black. She addressed him as Mr. Reed and found him to be very dignified. However, she was called out by the secretary that black men should never be addressed as "Mister". She continued calling him Mr. Reed, but the janitor kept his distance.

Another instance was when his mother came home one day from school and befriended a black girl. The other students threw stones at them and called his mother a "nigger lover". The next day,

186

Barack's grandfather took a leave from work, spoke to the principal, and reported the students who had thrown stones. The principal responded that white girls should not play with colored races.

Eventually, Barack's mother and father were married by a justice of the peace in a quiet ceremony; then, they moved to Hawaii. In Hawaii, there were many different cultures such as Japanese, Chinese, and Filipino. Racism was a thing of the past in Hawaii, and here is where the family became comfortable.

However, Barack still wondered why his father left. His mother and grandparents painted a picture of how amazing he was, but he still did not understand. He even found articles about his father and a photograph of him. Barack felt that something was amiss in his childhood and he grew older, not knowing his father.